Vengeance of the Lord

The Justice System of God

Dr. Bill Winston

Unless otherwise identified, Scripture quotations are from the King James Version (KJV) of the Bible.

Scripture quotations marked (NIV) are taken from The HOLY BIBLE® New International Version. Copyright © 1973, 1978, 1984, 2011 by Biblica, Inc.™ Used by permission of Zondervan. www.zondervan.com

Scripture quotations marked (KJ21) are taken from the 21st Century King James Version®. Copyright © 1994. Used by permission of Deuel Enterprises, Inc., Gary, SD 57237. All rights reserved.

Scripture quotations marked (MSG) are taken from The Message. Copyright © 1993, 1994, 1995, 1996, 2000, 2001, 2002. Used by permission of NavPress Publishing Group.

Scripture quotations marked (GNT) are taken from the Good News Translation® (Today's English Version, Second Edition) Copyright © 1992 American Bible Society. All rights reserved.

Scripture quotations marked (AMP) are taken from the Amplified® Bible. Copyright © 2015 by The Lockman Foundation, La Habra, CA 90631. All rights reserved. For permission to quote information visit http://www.lockman.org/

Scripture quotations marked (TLB) are taken from The Living Bible. Copyright © 1971 by Tyndale House Foundation. Used by permission of Tyndale House Publishers Inc., Carol Stream, Illinois 60188. All rights reserved. The Living Bible, TLB, and The Living Bible logo are registered trademarks of Tyndale House Publishers.

Scripture quotations marked (NKJV) are from the New King James Version®. Copyright © 1982 by Thomas Nelson. Used by permission. All rights reserved.

Scripture quotations marked (CEV) are taken from the Contemporary English Version® Copyright © 1995 American Bible Society. All rights reserved.

Scripture quotations marked (TJB) or The Jerusalem Bible are taken from The Jerusalem Bible®. Copyright ©1966, 2018 by Penguin Random House. Used by permission. All rights reserved.

Scripture quotations marked (NLT) are taken from the Holy Bible, New Living Translation. Copyright © 1996, 2004, 2007 by Tyndale House Foundation. Used by permission of Tyndale House Publishers, Inc., Carol Stream, Illinois 60188. All rights reserved.

Scripture quotations marked (AMPC) are taken from the Amplified® Bible, Classic Edition. Copyright © 1954, 1958, 1962, 1964, 1965, 1987 by The Lockman Foundation Used by permission. www.Lockman.org

Scripture quotations marked (MEV) are taken from The Holy Bible, Modern English Version. Copyright © 2014 by Military Bible Association. Published and distributed by Charisma House. Used by permission. All rights reserved.

Scripture quotations marked (TPT) are taken from The Passion Translation®. Copyright © 2017 by Broad Street Publishing® Group, LLC. Used by permission. All rights reserved. thePassionTranslation.com

Vengeance of the Lord: The Justice System of God

Bill Winston

ISBN: 978-1-63541-014-3

Copyright © 2019

All rights reserved

Published by Bill Winston Ministries

P.O. Box 947

Oak Park, IL 60303-0947

Contents and/or cover may not be reproduced in whole or in part in any form without the express written consent of the author or Bill Winston Ministries.

Printed in the United States of America

Contents

Introduction vii

Chapter 1 The Justice System of God 1

Chapter 2 A Fresh Oil Anointing 13

Chapter 3 Understanding Justice 17

Chapter 4 A Right View of Vengeance
 and Recompense 29

Chapter 5 Your Harvest is Crying Out 43

Chapter 6 Why We Need Vengeance 57

Chapter 7 Not a Martyr But a Savior 65

Conclusion 73

Prayer Confessions 83

Endnotes 93

Introduction

We are living in a time and season when the kingdom or a new government of God is being established throughout the earth. It's a time when every spiritual force that has been assisting the ungodly against God's end-time army of believers will now be put down. This is a part of what the Bible calls "the day of the Lord's vengeance *and* the year of recompences for the controversy of Zion" (Isaiah 34:8). *The Message* translation says, "It's God's scheduled time for vengeance, the year all Zion's accounts are settled." A time when Isaiah prophesies that the Lord will "comfort Zion"...when "mourning is turned to dancing." All that has been harassing or causing dishonor to the believers; everything standing against our lives, careers, businesses, fruitfulness, and making God's people uncomfortable will be removed. This season, which has already begun, is a time when the Church will be distinguished above all nations of the earth as she moves into her prophetic destiny of prominence and dominance. God says, "I will render vengeance to my enemies, and will reward them that hate me" (Deuteronomy 32:41).

This "vengeance of the Lord," or the judgment (justice) of God, is a vital part of kingdom manifestation, and the lack of its teaching is one of the main reasons why society has not reflected the Church's influence in the nations. In times when we should have been victorious in holding back iniquity, evil and darkness have been spreading at an alarming rate. And, because the vengeance of the

Lord has not been widely preached, many in the Body of Christ have been victims.

In the book of Isaiah it says, "Therefore my people are gone into captivity, because *they have* no knowledge..." (Isaiah 5:13).

Our kingdom authority and anointing gives us the power to regulate, legislate, enforce and establish God's rule and reign wherever we are sent. "The Lord said unto my Lord, Sit thou at my right hand, until I make thine enemies thy footstool" (Psalm 110:1).

We, the Church, cannot for a moment afford to shrink back from confronting evil or unjust laws of the land because of fear or "what will happen to me." Sir Winston Churchill once said, "The power of the wicked is always enhanced by the timidity and indecision of the righteous."[1]

In Daniel, chapter 6, Daniel defied King Darius' decree (a law) "that every man that shall ask *a petition* of any God or man within thirty days, save of thee, O king, shall be cast into the den of lions" (verse 12). "Now when Daniel knew that the writing was signed, he went into his house; and his windows being opened in his chamber toward Jerusalem, he kneeled upon his knees three times a day and prayed..." (verse 10). Daniel made an uncompromising stand against an ungodly law.

Daniel continued to honor his God by praying as he had always done despite the ungodly law of the Medes. He placed his total faith and trust in his God for everything he needed, including divine protection. The result was that Daniel was cast into the den of lions. Today we call that "capital punishment."

I think you remember the outcome. Daniel lived, being untouched, declaring, "God sent his angel to shut the mouths of the lions so that they would not hurt me. He did this because he knew that I was innocent and because I have not wronged you, Your Majesty" (Daniel 6:22 GNT). God had commanded vengeance on behalf of His servant Daniel "because he believed in his God." Then at the king's command, "...they brought those men which had accused Daniel, and they cast *them* into the den of lions, them, their children, and their wives; and the lions had the mastery of them, and brake all their bones..." (verse 24). This all happened without Daniel trying to fight his own battle or seek his own revenge. When men were out to destroy him, God promoted him and he grew in honor and prosperity.

Verse 23 in Daniel, chapter 6, reveals an important principle about the Lord's vengeance (emphasis mine).

> Then was the king exceeding glad for him, and commanded that they should take Daniel up out of the den. So Daniel was taken up out of the den, and no manner of hurt was found upon him, *because he believed in his God.*

Here's the principle. <u>The vengeance of the Lord is not automatic.</u> God has to work through a person who believes and has confidence in God's ability to execute judgment and justice. Daniel believed in his God and His power and sovereignty to deliver him from the lions—and God did.

Time to Shine

We are also in the time that the prophet Joel speaks about saying, "and my people shall never be ashamed." It is a time when systems, institutions, codes, cultures, laws and legislations will adjust to accommodate our divine purpose. And the "hand of the Lord" will be upon anyone who touches us or attempts to send out spells to sabotage our mission. We are untouchable and cannot be cursed. The psalmist declares this in Psalm 75:

> You have set a time to judge with fairness... You tell every bragger, "Stop bragging!" And to the wicked you say, "Don't boast of your power!...Our Lord and our God, victory doesn't come from the east or the west or from the desert. You are the one who judges. You can take away power and give it to others. Verses 2, 4, 6–7 CEV

The book of Isaiah declares this concerning us:

> But in that coming day no weapon turned against you will succeed. You will silence every voice raised up to accuse you. These benefits are enjoyed by the servants of the Lord; their vindication will come from me. I, the Lord, have spoken! Isaiah 54:17 NLT

This is our time to shine "the light of the glorious gospel of Christ" in every nation. It's time to take our place in our designated spheres of influence—not compete with the world but have dominion over it—providing leadership for those who are trapped in a world of darkness. Someone might say, "Well, I'm leaving my job and going into full-time ministry." Well, think again. You may already be in full-time ministry right there in that secular job.

We don't change the system by getting out of the system. To have kingdom impact, we cannot lock ourselves away in some monastery simply praying for

Introduction

"all those sinners out there." No. God positions us within the system and through His guidance and His anointing (power), we become the greatest influence in it. Both Joseph and Daniel were planted among astrologers, sorcerers and soothsayers, and they each rose up to change the whole system from the inside.

Recently, in this century, the justice system of the world has been one of the main targets of demonic abuse, and without the invasion of the kingdom and heaven's justice system, everything in society will eventually collapse. Why the justice system? I believe it's because it's the most efficient and effective way to shift a culture. When ungodly laws are passed and go unchallenged, they affect the thinking and behavior of the masses. People think wrong is right, causing entire nations to spiral into moral decline.

Let me make very clear that the vengeance of the Lord has nothing to do with hate, emotional resentment, or retaliation, but it involves the necessity of punishing offenders, which proceeds from a love of justice. This vengeance is the judgment of God upon the devil and his agents of evil, including anything and everything standing in the way of establishing God's kingdom or government. Those hindering or stopping the spread of the gospel and those interfering with the rights of God's kingdom citizens are subject to God's vengeance. Again, this vengeance is not about revenge that springs from enmity, bitterness, or ill will; which the Bible says are all works of the flesh...but from a love of justice.

God said to Abraham, "And I will bless (do good for, benefit) those who bless you, And I will curse [that is, subject to My wrath and judgment] the one who curses (despises, dishonors, has contempt for) you. And in you all the families (nations) of the earth will be blessed" (Genesis 12:3 AMP). Abraham's blessing pertains to us as the seed of Abraham. (See Galatians 3:13–14, 29; 4:28.)

The apostle Paul invoked vengeance on Elymas, the sorcerer, and he went blind, not by the influence (work) of the devil but by the injunction of the Holy Spirit.

> Then Saul (who also is called Paul), filled with the Holy Ghost, set his eyes on him and said, "O, full of all guile and all mischief, thou child of the devil, thou enemy of all righteousness, wilt thou not cease to pervert the right ways of the Lord? And now, behold, the hand of the Lord is upon thee, and thou shalt be blind, not seeing the sun for a season." Acts 13:9–11 KJ21

Make no mistake, God loves people. The Bible also says that "God is love" (1 John 4:8). The Lord declares in Ezekiel 33:11, "Say unto them, *As* I live, saith the Lord GOD, I have no pleasure in the death of the wicked; but that the wicked turn from his way and live...." God demonstrates His love for us in His plan of salvation through Jesus Christ, "For God so loved the world, that he gave his only begotten Son..." (John 3:16).

Jesus Christ redeemed us from the curse that came through Adam's fall declaring that "I came to save men's lives, not to destroy them" (Luke 9:46 paraphrased). But if people do not accept our Lord's overflowing grace that Jesus died to give us, they remain subject to the curse that is in the world and to the law of sin and death that still operates in the children of disobedience.

The bottom line, and one of the main reasons for writing this book, is that I believe that in these last days it will be impossible to fulfill your destiny without the

Introduction

vengeance of the Lord or, said another way, apart from the justice system of God clearing the way, the "greater works" will be impossible to manifest. This is what Jesus was referring to when He said in Luke 18:8, "I tell you that he will avenge them speedily. Nevertheless when the Son of man cometh, shall he find faith on the earth?" and also in Luke 21:22, "For these be the days of vengeance, that all things which are written may be fulfilled."

We are moving into a place and time unlike any before, a time of extreme darkness and gloominess. Yet, right from the midst of this darkness will emerge a great army of light, the Church, men and women of unquestionable integrity and unstoppable dominion whom nations will respect as they will decide the destinies of cities and continents. (See Joel 2:2, 11.) Armed with the "garments of vengeance," this army will not be found running away from trouble, but bringing trouble to the enemy and putting down every demonic work oppressing and troubling humanity.

> Justice was the LORD's armor; saving power was his helmet; anger and revenge were his clothes. Now the LORD will get furious and do to his enemies, both near and far, what they did to his people. He will attack like a flood in a mighty windstorm. Nations in the west and the east will then honor and praise his wonderful name. Isaiah 59:17–19 CEV

This is why the vengeance of the Lord must be preached. The covenant promises of God are not automatic; they require faith to operate or be released. People must believe and have faith in the Lord's vengeance to see its manifestation in their lives. Romans 10:17 tells us that "faith *cometh* by hearing, and hearing by the word of God." I decree that your faith in God's vengeance shall come as you read this book and whatever the destiny God has planned for you—it will be fulfilled, in Jesus' Name!

In closing, as you read this book, you will be armed with truth for unquestionable dominion and brought to a revelation of the power and resources available to you, enabling you to invoke and establish heaven's justice system in the world, wherever you are sent. The understanding of the Lord's vengeance brings confidence in God's ability and willingness to protect, preserve, prosper and promote you as you advance His kingdom agenda.

Righteous judgment is based on truth, and truth is what God says it is. The Spirit of Truth is the One who teaches us truth.

> Howbeit when he, the Spirit of truth, is come, he will guide you into all truth: for he shall not speak of himself; but whatsoever he shall hear, *that* shall he speak: and he will shew you things to come. John 16:13

Once we are born again, we have God-given authority to execute judgment and justice as part of our redemptive rights in Jesus Christ. We become judges for righteousness in the earth.

> Don't you know that God's people will judge the world? And if you are going to judge the world, can't you settle small problems? Don't you know that we will judge angels? And if that is so, we can surely judge everyday matters. I Corinthians 6:2–3 CEV

Introduction

Psalm 82 clearly outlines our responsibilities as righteous judges:

> How long will ye judge unjustly, and accept the persons of the wicked? Selah. Defend the poor and fatherless: do justice to the afflicted and needy. Deliver the poor and needy: rid *them* out of the hand of the wicked. They know not, neither will they understand; they walk on in darkness: all the foundations of the earth are out of course. I have said, Ye *are* gods; and all of you *are* children of the most High. Verses 2–6

Another translation says it this way:

> "How long will you judges refuse to listen to the voice of true justice and continue to corrupt what is right by judging in favor of the wrong?"

> "Defend the defenseless, the fatherless and the forgotten, the disenfranchised and the destitute. Your duty is to deliver the poor and the powerless; liberate them from the grasp of the wicked. But you continue in your darkness and ignorance while the foundations of society are shaken to the core! Didn't I commission you as judges, saying, 'You are all like gods, since you judge on my behalf. You are all like sons of the Most High, my representatives.' *The Passion Translation*

Finally, this message of the VENGEANCE OF THE LORD communicates supernatural courage when it is studied and a person is convinced of the Lord's vengeance to manifest. It is designed to give you boldness and a new attitude in the day of testing and to enable you to stand fearlessly and uncompromisingly in the face of extreme adversity, the same as Moses before Pharaoh or as Daniel and the three Hebrews before King Darius or the Babylonian King Nebuchadnezzar when they were confronted with unjust laws from an ungodly culture or system. I tell people, "What you know determines how far you go." In the book of Proverbs, it says, "A wise man *is* strong; yea, a man of knowledge increaseth strength," and "*If* thou faint in the day of adversity, thy strength *is* small" (Proverbs 24:5 and 10).

As you read this book, I decree, like the apostle Paul, that "the eyes of your understanding (are) enlightened; that ye may know what is the hope of his calling...and what *is* the **exceeding greatness of his power** to us-ward who believe..." (Ephesians 1:18–19 emphasis mine).

No matter what injustices or indignities you may have suffered in the past, know that the greatest power in the universe, Christ, is now in you and God Himself is watching over you, protecting and keeping your family and all that belongs to you. And one more thing, the Holy Spirit will not only provide you justice but also *recompense*, which means "to compensate, to return an equivalent amount or pay damages for anything given, done or suffered (unjustly)."[2] "For we know him that hath said, Vengeance *belongeth* unto me, I will recompense, saith the Lord. And again, The Lord shall judge his people" (Hebrews 10:30).

Enjoy!

Chapter 1

The Justice System of God

Justice is very important to God. In fact, it is the heart of God. If the enemy can destroy justice in somebody's life or in a government or nation, he can crush the hope and faith in the human heart and perpetuate every manner of evil.

American slavery, which allowed people to sell and own another human being based on the color of their skin, was once justified in the United States by law. The economy of the entire South was built upon it, affecting the thinking of millions of Americans for generations to come, even after slavery ended. This is one reason why the late Dr. Martin Luther King, Jr. in his famous "I Have a Dream" speech of 1963 referenced Amos 5:24. He was speaking to the nation about the terrible injustice of segregation and the denial of civil and legal rights for "Negroes" or African Americans. He said, "We will not be satisfied until justice rolls down like waters and righteousness like a mighty stream."[3]

I believe Dr. King had a revelation of God's justice and it caused a social revolution. It gave him uncommon boldness and fearlessness in the face of hate mail and death threats. But, where did God's justice originate from and why was it needed? To answer this, let's start in the Old Testament.

Abraham, Sarah and King Abimelech

God chose Abraham as the father of the faithful. He told him, "In you all the families (nations) of the earth will be blessed" (Genesis 12:3 AMP). The Bible says that Abraham believed God and "it was accounted to him for righteousness." Now, if anyone stood in the way of God's "high calling" for Abraham they were going to encounter God's vengeance. The Pharaoh of Egypt found this out when he took Sarai (before her name was changed to Sarah) into his house to be one of his concubines. "The Lord plagued Pharaoh and his house with great plagues because of Sarai, Abram's wife" (Genesis 12:14).

King Abimelech of Gerar also found this out when he took Sarah for himself into his palace, "But God came to Abimelech in a dream by night, and said to him, Behold, thou *art but* a dead man, for the woman which thou hast taken; for she *is* a man's wife...Now therefore restore the man *his* wife; for he *is* a prophet, and he shall pray for thee, and thou shalt live: and if thou restore *her* not, know thou that thou shalt surely die, thou, and all that *are* thine (all your people)" (Genesis 20:3, 7).

I believe that satan suspected that the family line of Abraham and Sarah had been chosen by God to bring forth the Deliverer (righteous Seed), that would "bruise his head," and he's now attempting to contaminate their gene pool. They had a divine mission the same way you and I are on a divine mission for God to establish His kingdom throughout the earth and to prepare for Jesus' return. We are here, divinely positioned, to bring to fruition what God had already planned beforehand,

and we are divinely protected by God's anointing, the Holy Spirit, who is with us, to execute vengeance upon all the enemies of God's people and nothing shall escape Him.

Not only did King Abimelech restore Abraham's wife, but the scriptures tell us that he told Abraham, "'Look my kingdom over, and choose the place where you want to live'...Then he turned to Sarah. 'Look,' he said, 'I am giving your "brother" (Abraham) a thousand silver pieces as damages for what I did, to compensate for any embarrassment and to settle any claim against me regarding this matter. **Now justice has been done**'" (Genesis 20:15–16 TLB emphasis mine).

The Bible goes on to say, "Then Abraham prayed, asking God to cure the king and queen and the other women of the household, so that they could have children; for God has stricken all the women with barrenness to punish Abimelech for taking Abraham's wife" (verses 17–18 TLB). God told the king in his dream that "he (Abraham) is a prophet, and he shall pray for thee, and thou shalt live." God needed His prophet to reverse the divine judgment that had been executed against Abimelech's household.

God will bring judgment upon your adversaries and in so doing He will punish and penalize them for what they have put you through. He will force them to compensate you for the damages that they caused you. Again, "Vengeance *belongeth* unto me, I will recompense, saith the Lord" (Hebrew 10:30).

As was mentioned in the introduction, *recompense* means "to compensate, pay damages, to make return of an equivalent for anything given, done or suffered; to make amends." So, whatever is afflicting or humiliating you, whatsoever is against your peace, progress, career, business or family, God is going to command vengeance upon them.

God Is the Judge

It took the vengeance of the Lord for Moses to enforce Israel's release from Egypt. Whatever or whoever was resisting Moses did not go unpunished. When it was time for the children of Israel to be delivered from Egypt, the Lord told Moses, "And I am sure that the king of Egypt will not let you go, no, not by a mighty hand. And I will stretch out my hand, and smite Egypt with all my wonders which I will do in the midst thereof: and after that he will let you go" (Exodus 3:19–20).

To fulfill God's mandate, Moses needed knowledge of God's "vengeance" to take his place of authority. He didn't go to Pharaoh or Egypt's court for permission. No. By faith, Moses invoked the justice system of God, the Supreme Court of the universe, and because of Pharaoh's resistance, the judgment started upon Egypt. Psalm 75:7 states, "But God *is* the judge: he putteth down one, and setteth up another." Isaiah 33:22 says, "For the LORD *is* our judge, the LORD *is* our lawgiver, the LORD *is* our king; he will save us."

Vengeance in the New Testament

It took vengeance for Joseph and Mary to stay in the plan of God regarding baby Jesus. After King Herod had heard that there was a king in his jurisdiction, he "...slew all the children that were in Bethlehem, and in all the coasts thereof, from two years old and under..." (Matthew 2:16). He didn't know that God had Joseph take Mary and

The Justice System of God

baby Jesus down to Egypt. The scriptures go on to say, "But when Herod was dead, behold, an angel of the Lord appeareth in a dream to Joseph in Egypt, saying, Arise, and take the young child and his mother, and go into the land of Israel: for they are dead which sought the young child's life" (verses 19–20).

Notice, this scripture still refers to Jesus as a young child. So, within a relatively short period of time, perhaps three or four years, Herod, and all his company who were resisting the plan of God to redeem mankind, were terminated. I decree, "Whatever is resisting God's plan for your life, whatever is tampering with your destiny is stopped today." Isaiah 61:2 promises that your day is here "...the day of vengeance of our God; to comfort all that mourn."

Examples of God's vengeance are also found in the book of Acts. Do you remember when Ananias and his wife Sapphira sold a piece of property and decided together to cheat and keep some of the money for themselves? "When Ananias took the rest of the money to the apostles, Peter said, 'Why has Satan made you keep back some of the money from the sale of the property? Why have you lied to the Holy Spirit? You lied to God!'" (Acts 5:3–4 CEV).

What happened? The scriptures say Ananias dropped dead on the spot, and men came in and carried away his body to bury it. Three hours later Sapphira came in, not knowing what had happened to her husband, and also lied.

> Then Peter said, "Why did the two of you agree to test the Lord's Spirit? The men who buried Ananias are by the door, and they will carry you out!" At once she fell at Peter's feet and died. Verses 9–10 CEV

Because they tried to deal deceitfully and lie to the Holy Ghost, the judgment of God fell on them. They surrendered their will to satan who is a liar and the father of lies (John 8:44).

Acts, chapter 13, gives another example of God's judgment that occurred when a false prophet and sorcerer named Bar-jesus (or Elymas) opposed Barnabas and Saul when they preached the Word of God to Sergius Paulus, the governor of Paphos. The governor, who had great influence, had asked to hear the gospel, but the sorcerer was blocking this from happening.

> Then Saul—also known as Paul—was filled with the Holy Spirit; he looked straight at the magician (sorcerer) and said, 'You son of the Devil! You are the enemy of everything that is good...The Lord's hand will come down on you now; you will be blind and will not see the light of day for a time.' At once Elymas felt a dark mist cover his eyes.... Acts 13:9–11 GNT

This false prophet was trying to stop the advancement of the gospel, but God's vengeance removed the apostles' adversary. God knows that satan is our true adversary, and that he uses people, especially those outside of God's covenant, to frustrate and fight God's servants and hinder them from carrying out His instructions.

We must remember that our enemy is never flesh and blood. Our true warfare is never with what we can see or feel. This is why vengeance only operates *supernaturally* by faith. The story of General George Patton fighting the Nazis during WWII is a great example of this principle.

During a critical battle of the war, General Patton knew that he needed God's intervention to win or countless lives and peace for the world would be lost. Rains were steadily falling and heavy fog was stopping the Allied Forces from advancing against the German soldiers. He told his chaplain, James H. O'Neill, "We must ask God to stop these rains. These rains are the margin that hold defeat or victory." Patton wanted to invoke the "hand of the Lord" to move on his behalf. He prayed a prayer for good weather written by Chaplain O'Neill. He also had every man under his command pray it. The next day the weather was clear and perfect. His men went forward and won the battle.[4]

Notice, General Patton wasn't being "religious" when he asked Chaplain O'Neill to write a prayer for good weather so they could win the battle. He obviously wasn't thinking, "Well, it must be the Lord's will that it's raining." Or, "God must be punishing us with this rain because He is mad at us." No. He went "boldly to the throne of grace" and asked God's help to secure his victory.

The vengeance of the Lord is one of our covenant rights, but because vengeance has not been taught in the Body of Christ, many Christians end up fighting their own battles instead of resting in the assurance of God's deliverance and vindication. The Bible says that "My people are destroyed for lack of knowledge." This says to me that Christians have some knowledge but not enough. And the knowledge we need most is *revelation* knowledge, which comes from the Spirit of God. Pastors, teachers and evangelists must begin to preach and teach about the vengeance of the Lord so that their people can have the faith to put it into operation. As Romans 10:14 and 17 says, "How then shall they call on him in whom they have not believed? and how shall they believe in him of whom they have not heard? and how shall they hear without a preacher?...So then faith *cometh* by hearing, and hearing by the word of God." In so many cases, as I shared earlier, because we have not known vengeance, we have been victims. We must know and believe as a present real fact that we have been delivered. Any blessings which are recovered must be by faith. You must believe you have it before you see it—before it is manifested.

God Is Finishing What He Started

In the book of Genesis, God commanded Adam to "be fruitful, and multiply, and replenish the earth." This meant that Adam was to spread the garden of Eden, its beauty, opulence and culture, throughout the whole earth. When Adam and Eve fell from sin and lost their communion with God, they began to create another culture outside of God and God's original thinking. It became a culture based on fallen man's thinking and not on the principles and laws of the government of God.

When Jesus came, He reintroduced the kingdom of God that operated in the Garden, and put mankind back on track with Adam's original assignment. At the age of thirty, Jesus declares His ministry when He stands in the synagogue to read part of Isaiah 61: "The Spirit of the Lord *is* upon me, because he hath anointed me to preach the gospel to the poor; he hath sent me to heal the brokenhearted, to preach deliverance to the captives, and recovering of sight to the blind, to set at liberty them that are bruised, to preach the acceptable year of the Lord. And he closed the book..." (Luke 4:18–20). Jesus intentionally left out "the day of vengeance of our God" in Isaiah 61:2.

Why? The vengeance of the Lord was not part of Jesus' ministry on the earth. Vengeance and recompense would become the ministry of the Holy Spirit after the day of Pentecost. Through the power of the Holy Spirit, who lives on the inside of every born-again believer, we have now stepped into the part that Jesus left out, "...the day of vengeance of our God; to comfort all that mourn... ye shall eat (consume or devour) the riches (wealth or substance) of the Gentiles, and in their glory shall ye boast yourselves" (Isaiah 61:2, 6).

Through vengeance, or God's justice system, we will see the complete plan of God manifested. The Church, as an institution, will be recognized as the mightiest and wealthiest in the world. By His anointing, God is beautifying the Church and destroying every work of the wicked one.

As comfort comes to the Church, judgment will come to the world system bringing the greatest transfer of wealth ever seen. There will be such prosperity in the Body of Christ that it will stagger the imagination of the world. Isaiah 60 says, "...the LORD shall arise upon thee (His people)" and the "wealth of the nations shall be converted (overturned) unto thee" (verses 2 and 5 GNT, KJV).

God Protects You

The vengeance of the Lord is designed to protect you, your family, your business, your church and everything that you own or are involved in. As you move forward, possessing your inheritance and fulfilling your God-given assignment, our God will judge anyone, any system, or any army that tries to touch you or interfere with your assignment. (See 2 Kings 19.)

When Southern newspapers widely published that Booker T. Washington, the founder of Tuskegee Institute (today's Tuskegee University), dined at the White House at the invitation of President Theodore "Teddy" Roosevelt, many white Southerners were outraged.

"During the furore over this incident both the President and Mr. Washington received many threats against their lives. The President had the Secret Service to protect him, while Mr. Washington had no such reliance."[5] During this period it is reported that Washington received "enough threatening letters to fill a desk drawer."[6]

Some years later it was discovered that one of these threats led to "a hired assassin"[7] visiting Tuskegee for the purpose of murdering Booker T. Washington. Here is a brief written account.

> A strange Negro was hurt in jumping off the train before it reached Tuskegee Institute station. There being no hospital for Negroes in the town of Tuskegee he was taken to the hospital of the Institute, where he was cared for and nursed for several weeks before he was able to leave. Mr. Washington was absent in the North during all of this time.
>
> Many months later this Negro confessed that he had come to Tuskegee in the pay of a group of white men in Louisiana for the purpose of assassinating Booker Washington.[8]

It is written that the man became so ashamed while being cared for by the medical and nursing staff employed by his intended target that as soon as he was able he left town before Washington returned, unable to carry out his wicked plan.[9]

Washington would go on to make Tuskegee Institute "one of the most successful schools in the South."[10] In 1905, the school "turned out more self-made millionaires than Yale, Harvard and Princeton universities combined,"[11] and "by 1915 Washington had built Tuskegee into a school of 107 buildings on 2,000 acres with over 1,500 students and more than 200 teachers and professors."[12]

You are God's property which means you can no longer be molested, tormented, assaulted, or harassed or killed. Zechariah 2:8 says, "...for he that toucheth you toucheth the apple of his eye." You are the "apple of God's eye."

This word *apple* in Hebrew translates "pupil."[13] Have you ever tried to touch the pupil of your eye? You can't. Your eyelid immediately closes to protect it. It's the same with our relationship with God, especially when we are actively advancing His kingdom. If anyone tries to harm or hurt you, God's presence will cover and protect you. But you have to believe this. Everything in the kingdom is received according to your faith.

I decree that whatever has been blocking God's plan from coming to pass in your life is now being removed! Everything held up that was prepared by God for your destiny must be released now... in Jesus' Name!

Now is your set time and season. No more delays, denials, or substitutes, and wherever the enemy has been holding you back, you are breaking forth! The justice system of God is now executing vengeance on your behalf. Your responsibility is to believe this.

Chapter 2

A Fresh Oil Anointing

Psalm 92:10–11 says, "But my horn shalt thou exalt like *the horn of* an unicorn: I shall be anointed with fresh oil. Mine eye also shall see *my desire* on mine enemies, *and* mine ears shall hear *my desire* of the wicked that rise up against me."

There is coming a new anointing, which the Bible calls "fresh oil," to empower the end-time Church to fulfill its prophetic destiny, to finish the dominion mandate God gave to Adam..."Be fruitful and multiply, and replenish the earth, and subdue it." This will be at a time, as one man said, "When Christian people will be the most attractive people in society." Part of this anointing is for the Holy Spirit to execute vengeance on all of your adversaries.

Some ministries are trying to get by on the old oil of yesteryear's anointing (the old wine), but God has fresh oil, a new anointing, that will raise up a nation of kings and priests to fill the whole earth with the kingdom of God. Get ready for the "fresh oil"!

Some clergy and lay people may think that this revelation of God's vengeance is not true or something only for the Old Testament. But, by the authority of God's Word, it is true and it is for today. Once Jesus was raised from the dead and was seated at the right hand of the Father, His ministry was completely handed over to the person of the Holy Spirit. And, as mentioned earlier, one of the jobs of the Holy Spirit is to execute vengeance on behalf of the people of God. In the book of Psalms, we find: "The LORD works righteousness and justice for all the oppressed" (Psalm 103:6 NIV). In the book of Hebrews, the Lord says, "Vengeance *belongeth* unto me, I will recompense, saith the Lord." And again, The Lord shall judge his people" (Hebrews 10:30).

My Personal Encounter with Vengeance

I personally experienced the vengeance of the Lord when we acquired our shopping mall and worship center many years ago. One Sunday when leaving church, God told me to "buy that mall" which was located across the street from where we were temporarily holding our worship services. In obedience to this direct, "rhema word" (revelation) from the Lord, I proceeded to pursue its purchase.

The church had just signed the deal, with the help of a small minority bank on the South Side of Chicago, and paid our money to the previous owners when, without warning, the local village officials told us that we would not be able to hold our worship services in the complex. I asked a legal professional what we should do, and he advised me to sue the Village. I asked him how long that would take, and his answer was "about five years." The problem was that our entire congregation was preparing to meet there for the mid-week evening service the next night. Then, I asked someone who was in real estate what I should do and he suggested that I find another location on the North Side of Chicago to hold services temporarily. I knew that neither of those suggestions was God's best.

The next day was New Year's Eve and the church needed a place to hold services that night. It was (seemingly) an impossible situation.

Early that morning, I began praying in the Spirit to receive wisdom and direction from the Lord on how to handle the situation. Understand, as Christians, we have the ability to be informed on another level. We were expecting crowds of people to attend, especially because many thought this mall purchase was impossible. In answer to my prayer, the Lord gave me some very specific instructions—what I call "Faith Steps."

He said, "Call a meeting with the Village mayor. Read a specific portion of Romans, chapter 13, to her and emphasize that she is a minister." The Lord also directed me to type the scriptures using a large font so I could easily read these verses to the mayor. In obedience, I followed these directions exactly as the Lord gave them.

I pushed to get a meeting with the mayor around noon, I began reading Romans 13 just as the Lord had directed. While I was reading the scriptures, the Spirit began to move on her heart. She shared with me that the Village board had already voted "no," which meant that we couldn't hold service in the mall complex for New Year's Eve. The mayor then asked if she could call me in a couple of hours. She said she wanted to call the members of the city council to discuss the matter. I left, and about two hours later, the mayor called my office to say that she was not able to locate any council members, but would approve our worship service there for one night only and would keep the police away.

Although she said, "for one night," I knew that God had opened a door for our church that no man could shut. We received a 24-hour breakthrough. It was the day of the Lord's vengeance!

By trusting in the Lord, there was no need for me to get emotional and say or do something that could cause more problems later and bring a reproach upon the church of Jesus Christ. I followed the Lord's instructions and allowed Him to fight our battle. As a result, we held our service in the mall that night and have been praising God there ever since. God is a master strategist. Once the door opened, the Village ordinances were changed to permit our church to have permanent residence on the mall property. Since that time, we have built a state-of-the-art facility and contributed millions of dollars of state and local revenues through property and sales taxes.

My experience is a clear example of why we must seek the Lord in every battle we face. Only when we hear God's voice and receive His wisdom and instructions will we have the necessary faith and boldness to confront unjust decrees and say "thus saith the Lord." Realize, it wasn't the people but the devil attempting to block our ministry's progress and he was defeated by the vengeance of the Lord. This is why God's people can live with confidence in these last days, no matter how impossible our situations may seem. **I declare whatever has been resisting God's plan for your life, your ministry or your business is stopped today, in Jesus' Name!"**

Chapter 3

Understanding Justice

The Holy Spirit wants to partner with each one of us. The apostle Paul brings this out when he writes "...the communion of the Holy Ghost, (will) *be* with you all. Amen." The word *communion* in the Greek is the word *koinónia,* where we get the word "partnership."[14] An example of this is in Luke 5 where Simon Peter, at Jesus' command, went back out to go fishing and couldn't handle the supernatural catch (draught) of fish alone (verse 7). He called for his partners to come and help him.

The Holy Spirit wants to assume a greater responsibility for you in this world. He wants a new level of relationship with us if for no other reason but to guide us around demonic "minefields" and to bring us out of life-threatening situations. For instance, the Holy Spirit directed the apostle Paul's missionary journeys: "After they were come to Mysia, They assayed to go to Bithynia; but the Spirit suffered them not" (Acts 16:7). The *Amplified Bible* says "did not permit them" and *The Message* translation says "Their plan was to turn west into Asia Province, but the Holy Spirit blocked that route...(they) tried to go north to Bithynia, but the Spirit of Jesus wouldn't let them go there either" (verses 6–8).

The Holy Spirit wants to partner with you and assume a greater responsibility for your life in this world.

When you know that one of the main jobs of the Holy Spirit in these last days is to execute God's vengeance upon all of the enemies of God's people, and nothing shall escape Him, it will give you a new level of boldness in your kingdom assignment. Remember, knowledge is the principle source of strength (Proverbs 24:5, 10). It will create a significant change in your attitude and behavior. And like Moses, you will no longer have to take "no" for an answer!

This is why understanding justice and trusting in the vengeance of the Lord is so important in carrying out the plans of transforming this world that God has for you in these last days. So, let's go deeper into this discussion.

The Need for Justice

> And judgment is turned away backward, and justice standeth afar off: for truth is fallen in the street, and equity cannot enter. Yea, truth faileth; and he *that* departeth from evil maketh himself a prey.... Isaiah 59:14–15

Many people lose all hope when justice does not go forth in a land or nation. And when people lose hope, they also lose faith and open themselves up to all kinds of evil coming into their lives and into their nation. Why? Because faith is the only force that can stop the devil.

This is why the justice systems of earthly governments must come back in line with the way it is in heaven, and why the vengeance of the Lord must be preached. This is the Church's responsibility. Only the gospel can restore people's hope and faith in God and stop the spread of darkness caused by unjust systems of demonic abuse. Faith in God's justice system is missing in much of the world, and it's time for the Church to bring it back. Let me share some examples of why faith in the vengeance of the Lord is needed now more than ever.

A Cry for Racial Justice

When I was a boy growing up in Tuskegee, Alabama, the home of the historic Moton Field where the Tuskegee Airmen were trained to fly, African Americans could not swim in the same public swimming pools that whites swam in. We could not go to their schools or eat in their restaurants or attend the same movie theaters. We could not even attend their churches, because if we did, we would probably have been put out or arrested. Racial segregation was the law of the land.

This racial inequality and injustice in America led to a Civil Rights Movement that spread throughout the South and soon the nation. Although the "movement" was nonviolent, the protests often led to violent clashes with southern police and local white residents. Then, when its leader, Dr. Martin Luther King, Jr., was assassinated in Memphis, Tennessee, riots broke out in many urban areas across America. Many blacks took to the streets in anger and despair because they had lost all hope that justice would ever come. Many feel this same injustice and despair today. The problem is that it is not a natural problem. It is a spiritual problem that requires a spiritual solution.

For example in 2017, a young white woman was killed and over thirty people were injured when a twenty-year-old white man drove his car into a group of people protesting an alt-right rally of Neo-Nazis, Ku Klux Klan members and white nationalists in Charlottesville, Virginia. Peaceful protests across the nation were organized to "denounce the hateful speech" spoken in Charlottesville. There was a cry for racial hatred and injustice to stop.[15]

Many people are questioning if there will ever be justice for people of color in America? Will Dr. King's dream ever manifest..."that my four little children will one day live in a nation where they will not be judged by the color of their skin but by the content of their character?"[16]

The answer lies not with the government of the United States, but with the government of God, and Dr. Martin Luther King, Jr. understood this. He knew that to bring societal transformation, he needed an authority more powerful than the political strongman and legal systems that ruled Alabama and the entire South during his day. Through Amos 5:24, Dr. King called on God as the Judge, whom Abraham called "the Judge of all the earth" (Genesis 18:25).

Now we, as the Church, must have the same faith as Dr. King to end racial injustice today. This Judge requires the faith of the believer before He can and will execute judgment. In Psalm 82:2, God says, "How long will you judge unjustly and accept the persons of the wicked." Another translation says, "How long will you keep judging unfairly and favoring evil people" (CEV).

We must declare like Dr. Martin Luther King Jr., "But let justice run down like waters And righteousness like an ever-flowing stream [flowing abundantly]" (Amos 5:24 AMP).

Race and Poverty

When I was young boy in Alabama, many blacks didn't go to court because there was no justice there. Often

Understanding Justice

people would be judged guilty no matter if they were innocent or they were the victim.

Unfortunately, too many people in America and other countries have experienced unfair treatment and abuse at the hand of our criminal justice system. Sadly, race and poverty often affect how justice is dispensed.

This was the case of Anthony Ray Hinton, a poor black man in rural Alabama who spent nearly thirty years on death row after being wrongly convicted of two murders he didn't commit. His story is chronicled in the book *The Sun Does Shine:*

> ...with no money and a different system of justice for a poor black man in the South, Hinton was sentenced to death by electrocution. He spent the first three years on death row at Holman State Prison (in Alabama) in agonizing silence, full of despair and anger toward all who would send an innocent man to his death.[17]

Through prayer and the almost-eighteen-year effort of his defense attorney, who Hinton called "God's best lawyer"[18] (the professional shortcomings of his original public defender led to his conviction), Hinton was released in 2015. He was arrested in 1985.[19]

Stories like Hinton's are why many people, especially young African Americans, become disillusioned and even violent. Some rappers have even written songs about cop-killings and other types of revenge. In no way do I condone this type of music. These songs only make matters worse for the listener and for society. I do understand, however, the loss of hope and the sense of powerlessness behind them, and the desire to execute their own justice.

Vengeance of the Lord

The Bible says, "There is a way *that seems* right to a man, But its end *is* the way of death" (Proverbs 14:12 NKJV). No matter how angry we might feel, we cannot give into rage and revenge. Perhaps the words spoken by Anthony Ray Hinton after his conviction was overturned and he won his freedom, say it best, "I forgive them...I chose to forgive. I chose to stay vigilant to any signs of anger or hate in my heart. They (the State of Alabama) took thirty years of my life. If I couldn't forgive, if I couldn't feel joy, that would be like giving them the rest of my life. The rest of my life is mine."[20]

The apostle Paul wrote in Romans 12:19 KJ21, "Dearly beloved, avenge not yourselves, but rather give place unto wrath; for it is written: 'Vengeance is Mine; I will repay, saith the Lord.'" Paul knew quite a bit about the injustice done to the first followers of Jesus Christ. You might say he had a front-row seat.

Before his conversion on the Damascus road, Paul was the Early Church's greatest enemy, hauling Christians off to jail for their faith. "Meanwhile, Saul was still breathing out murderous threats against the Lord's disciples. He went to the high priest and asked him for letters to the synagogues in Damascus, so that if he found any there who belonged to the Way, whether men or women, he might take them as prisoners to Jerusalem" (Acts 9:1–2 NIV).

Paul's persecution of the Church was well known throughout Israel...until he has a supernatural encounter with Jesus. Paul learns about the Lord's love of justice for His people. "As he neared Damascus on his journey, suddenly a light from heaven flashed around him. He fell to the ground and heard a voice say to him, 'Saul, Saul, why do you persecute me?'" (verse 3). When Paul asks who is speaking, the voice answers, "I am

Jesus, whom you are persecuting...Now get up and go into the city, and you will be told what you must do" (verses 5–6).

When Paul got up from the ground he couldn't see and had to be led into Damascus by the men traveling with him. The scripture says, "For three days he (Paul) was blind, and did not eat or drink anything" (verse 9).

My point is this: You don't have to depend on the police or the court system to receive justice—you can go to the Supreme Court of heaven. God is the Judge.

Freedom to Preach the Gospel

This message on God's justice isn't only for people of color. It is for every believer in the family of God. As in the days of Daniel, the devil tries to influence governments to pass unjust laws that prevent Christians from worshipping God and following His Word, no matter their color or country. Let me share a story that made international news to support this.

In 2007, a Dutch pastor living in the Netherlands, was arrested under the suspicion that he was "inciting (child) abuse" because of a sermon that he had preached in his church. The news media reported that in his message he had "advocated spanking children as a parenting technique and said he occasionally hit his own children with a wooden spoon."[21] The problem: Spanking children, even your own, is against the law in the Netherlands.

In his message, the pastor had referenced Proverbs 13:24, "He that spareth his rod hated his son: but he that loveth him chasteneth him betimes." A news story reported, "The police put the preacher's children under the supervision of the Dutch child protection agency and questioned him...(however) based on the results of the investigation, the public prosecutor subsequently decided to refrain from further legal action."[22]

An important part of the pastor's story never made it in the news. The pastor later shared that while he was being detained in jail, he remembered my teaching on "Vengeance and Recompense." He remembered that God would defend and protect those who stand for righteousness and fight their battle. He said the message emboldened him to stand for the gospel and not compromise. He prayed for God's protection and deliverance and the police released him.

When the Laws of Heaven and Earth Collide

Remember, because vengeance operates by faith, God will not step in until we open our mouths boldly. Every time we speak boldly, we commit God to manifest openly. David spoke to the Philistine giant and before two armies, "This day the LORD will deliver you into my hand...." When threatened with execution, the three Hebrews came into agreement and boldly said the "God whom we serve is able to deliver us from the burning fiery furnace, and he will deliver *us* out of thine hand, O king." Not only did the Lord deliver and protect them, but the men that took them into the furnace were slain by the fire.

Sometimes the laws of earthly governments conflict with the laws of God. However, we must be like the three Hebrews in the book of Daniel who refused to compromise or "fall down and worship the golden image that Nebuchadnezzar the king hath set up." We must keep our trust in God. When we stand our ground and declare by faith what will happen, based on the laws of heaven, God is free to execute the judgment written. (See Psalm 149:9.)

Again, the vengeance of the Lord is not about trusting or relying on an earthly Babylonian court for justice but to trust only in Almighty God and the Supreme Court of the universe. In the book of Psalms, it is written, "For promotion *cometh* neither from the east, nor from the west, nor from the south. But God *is* the judge" (Psalm 75:6–7). The *New Living Translation* says this, "It is God alone who judges; he decides who will rise and who will fall."

In some way or another, the devil has harassed and stolen from many of God's people, everything from health and long life to marriages and millionaire status. Well, that time is over. God is now saying, "I'm going to restore to you the years"...there is an anointing for restoration. The days of your struggling are over! You are not going to have to struggle for anything else. As a matter of fact, anything from now on that is making you uncomfortable, God is going to remove it. And whatever has been interfering with your destiny, resisting God's plan for your life or holding you back, I command it to let you go!

Whatever will not let God's plan come to pass in your life is now being removed. Things that are against your peace, your promotion, your progress and prosperity... God will command vengeance to operate on your behalf.

The Need for Economic Justice

My last example of why we need heaven's justice to invade the earth is to bring economic justice. Proverbs 13:22 says, A good *man* leaveth an inheritance to his children's children: and the wealth of the sinner *is* laid up for the just." Let's focus on the last part of this verse.

God's Word says that the wealth of the sinner (those under satan's influence and who are controlling the world's wealth through his kingdom of darkness) is laid up for the just. One translation says "for the hands of the righteous" (AMP). This is God's truth, but I can guarantee you that satan will not give up the wealth he's stolen without a fight. Money is the source of his power and influence, and like Pharaoh, he only bows to power stronger than his.

Systemic poverty is an example of this. One man defined *systemic poverty* as "something that most people are born into and their fate is dictated and controlled by it...It deprives masses of people of their daily bread by stealing the fruit of their labor and keeping them in social misery."[23]

Look at the poor around the world who don't have enough to eat on a daily basis. Well-meaning governments, charities and corporations can send food and supplies to these countries, but if the country's distribution system fails to get the food to the people, they will remain in want and some may even die.

This is what happened in Haiti. Plenty of food and supplies were being shipped there, but they were not being distributed to the people. The news media reported that the food shortage had become so severe that some Haitians were even feeding their children mud. This is when someone should say, "Enough is enough!"

Poverty affects a person's total quality of life. It also affects their identity and sense of self-worth. Children who are chronically hungry and malnourished won't even go out to play. They have no joy. Many mothers who live in poverty can't even breastfeed because they can't produce sufficient breast milk. At the same time this is happening, some governments are paying farmers not to grow food. Something is wrong with this system!

In 2016, a respected prophet and teacher who disciples nations in the areas of prayer and the prophetic, Cindy Jacobs, spoke at one of our ministry conferences in Chicago. She shared that while she was in her hotel room, she was looking at the Forbes list of the wealthiest people in Chicago and there was not one African-American face on the list. Then she said, "That is a crime! It's not about black and white. It's about justice!"

Why did she say justice? Because there are demonic forces of darkness not only controlling the city of Chicago, but the economic systems of entire nations, and for one purpose: to hold the wealth among a chosen few. Satan has devised demonic systems and structures to keep the majority of people fighting each other and in a constant struggle for money simply to survive—both generationally and globally. But, God is about to change this!

Here is part of the prophetic word that Cindy Jacobs also gave during our conference:

> And the Lord says, "I am getting ready to do a new thing." God says, "Even in this room there are people that are going to be on the Forbes list of some of the wealthiest people in Chicago," says the Lord.
>
> And the Lord says, "Some of you have had a spiritual ambition to be millionaires," but God says, "Don't set your sights too low!" For God says, "Am I not able to make billionaires and not just millionaires?"

For the Lord says, "I want to give the Body of Christ the influence that you need to heal America and to heal this city," says the Lord.

And the Lord says, "I love the city of Chicago and I look down from heaven and see how satan is trying to stain the reputation of this city that I love." But God says, "I am going to raise up a new generation. I am going to raise up a new voice. There's a new sheriff in town!" (*To read the complete prophecy, see the Appendix*)

God is a God of justice, and I believe He is saying: "I am fed up with people dying because they can't eat. I'm fed up with hunger and poverty on this earth, and with people oppressing other people out of greed."
Vengeance is coming.

Chapter 4

A Right View of Vengeance and Recompense

God manifests His heart for justice through vengeance and recompense. Dr. Martin Luther King, Jr. often quoted, "But let justice run down like waters and righteousness like an ever-flowing stream [flowing abundantly]" (Amos 5:24 AMP). The *Amplified Bible* also says in Psalm 103:6, "The Lord executes righteousness and justice for all the oppressed."

As I shared earlier, God's vengeance has nothing to do with hate, resentment or emotional retaliation. It is God's judgment on people, systems and governments that are standing in the way of establishing His kingdom or are interfering with the rights and welfare of His people.

Hear what God spoke to Jacob in a dream saying: "For I have seen all that Laban has been doing to you" (Genesis 31:12 AMP). Long story short, Jacob, after 20 years of unjust servitude, ended up becoming very rich and taking everything Laban had. Let's look again at Hebrews 10:30, "For we know him that hath said, Vengeance *belongeth* unto me, I will recompense, saith the Lord. And again, The Lord shall judge his people."

Who is the "me" in this passage? God. And who will recompense? God. He is the One who will enact the vengeance and recompense in the world—not us. In fact, if we tried, we would probably only get in God's way and make things worse. Also, God knows that the entire demon-driven system is corrupt and that satan will always try to tip the scales of justice in his favor. And unless forced to, he will not surrender what was stolen or loosen his demonic grip of oppression.

Moses is a good example of this. When Moses was beginning to come alive to his calling in Exodus, chapter 2, he looked upon the burden of his people and saw an Egyptian beating a Hebrew. He took vengeance into his own hands and killed the Egyptian, burying him in the sand. Moses thought nobody saw him do it, but they did. (See verses 12–14.)

When Pharaoh found out about it, he wanted to slay Moses. What did Moses do? He left town and settled in the land of Midian on the backside of the mountain, afraid for his life.

After 40 years pass, God calls Moses to go back to Egypt to deliver the children of Israel out of slavery. Moses is supposed to bring them out of Egypt into the Promised Land, but because he is afraid that Pharaoh still wants to kill him, he starts giving God excuses why he isn't the one to do it: "Pardon your servant, Lord. I have never been eloquent...I am slow of speech and tongue" (Exodus 4:10 NIV).

In response, God decides to give Moses a demonstration of His power. He tells Moses to put his hand in his bosom, and when he pulls it out his hand is leprous. Then he tells Moses to put his hand back in. When Moses pulls it out the second time, it is clean. To further demonstrate His power, God tells Moses to throw his rod on the ground, and it turns into a snake. Then he tells Moses to pick up the snake by the tail and it turns back into a rod.

What was God doing? He was building Moses' confidence and faith in His supernatural power and might which nothing in heaven and earth can resist or withstand. As one man of God put it, "No one can say 'no' to God." Again, when we have a revelation of God's immense and unlimited power to execute vengeance on our behalf, it will significantly alter our attitude and behavior. It will give us uncommon boldness to confront unjust leaders and authority figures, no matter how powerful, who are standing in the way of God's plan and our kingdom assignment.

Moses didn't have an earthly army to confront and convince Pharaoh, one of the most powerful kings of his day, to let God's people go. No. He only had a walking stick, his brother Aaron...and Almighty God! Because God had appointed Moses and anointed him, Moses could stand boldly before the throne of Pharaoh and demand that Pharaoh release the children of Israel. This is what knowledge of the Lord's vengeance will do. It will embolden you to do the work of God without fear.

In the Lions' Den

Daniel is another example of how trusting God gives one the courage to obey God's commands even when threatened with capital punishment. King Darius had appointed three presidents over his kingdom and Daniel was one of them. His colleagues were very jealous of Daniel and plotted against him saying, "We shall not find any occasion against this Daniel, except we find *it* against him concerning the law of his God" (Daniel 6:5).

Daniel's enemies were counting on this: If they made a law that went against God's commandments, and Daniel bowed down to it, then Daniel would lose his power. And if Daniel stood up against that ungodly law and refused to bow to it, he would lose his life.

So they tricked the king into signing a decree that "whosoever shall ask a petition of any God or man for thirty days, save of thee, O king, he shall be cast into the den of lions" (verse 7). But when Daniel knew that the decree had been signed, he continued to pray three times a day as he always did before.

The other rulers told the king who had no choice but to throw Daniel into the lions' den because, according the law of the Medes and Persians, no decree or statute established by the king could be changed. So, Daniel was thrown in, and King Darius "returned to his palace and went to bed without dinner. He refused his usual entertainment and didn't sleep all night" (verse 18 TLB).

But look what happens in the morning.

> Then the king arose at dawn, at the break of day, and hurried to the den of lions. When he had come near the den, he called out to Daniel with a troubled voice. The king said to Daniel, "O Daniel, servant of the living God, has your God, whom you constantly serve, been able to rescue you from the lions?" Verses 19–20 AMP

Daniel's response? "Then Daniel said unto the king, O king, live forever" (verse 21). Through deception and deceit, Daniel was thrown, literally, to the lions to be eaten, but he responds to the king without anger or bitterness. Instead, Daniel tells him to live forever! "...So Daniel was taken up out of the den, and no manner of hurt was found upon him, because **he believed in his God**" (Daniel 6:23 emphasis mine).

Daniel's enemies never considered the power of Daniel's God to defend and deliver him through the vengeance of the Lord. Like Abraham, Daniel "believed in his God" and received protection and vindication! If Daniel had depended on human revenge, and stepped out of love and into hate, he probably would have been eaten by the lions and the justice system of God would not have prevailed.

Daniel's deliverance is not the end of the story. The king ordered all the men who had plotted against Daniel, plus their wives and children, to be thrown into the den of lions and before they could reach the bottom of the den, "the lions overpowered them and crushed all their bones" (verse 24 AMP).

Then the king made a new decree:

> Then King Darius wrote unto all people, nations, and languages that dwell in all the earth…I make a decree that in every dominion of my kingdom men tremble and fear before the God of Daniel. For He is the living God and steadfast for ever, and His Kingdom, that which shall not be destroyed, and His dominion shall be even unto the end. He delivereth and rescueth, and He worketh signs and wonders in heaven and in earth, who hath delivered Daniel from the power of the lions. Verses 25–27 KJ21

The Bible says that "From then on, Daniel was treated well (prospered) during the reign of Darius, and also in the following reign of Cyrus the Persian" (verse 28 MSG).

A Heritage of Protection

Remember what I said in an earlier chapter: When we are divinely positioned, we are divinely protected. Abraham and Sarah were divinely protected, twice. Moses was divinely protected from Pharaoh, and Daniel was divinely protected from jealous colleagues. And, as children of God, we and our families are divinely protected as we follow God and obey His commands.

We have a heritage of protection. Colossians 1:13 says, "who (God) hath delivered us from the power of darkness, and hath translated *us* into the kingdom of his dear Son." Again, this protection makes it impossible for you to be assaulted, molested, hurt (including accidents), or even harassed. God delivers your soul from destruction, "who redeemeth thy life from destruction; who crowneth thee with lovingkindness and tender mercies" (Psalm 103:4).

The Holy Spirit has sealed you against all the works of the wicked. We are sealed until the time our earthly assignment and pilgrimage are over. One of the reasons for the vengeance of the Lord is to bring us into the place prepared for us, and to guarantee that our destiny is reached.

God Repays You

God not only turns wrongs into rights, He also repays you for the wrongs you have suffered. It's called *recompense*, which, as we defined earlier, means to make return of an equivalent for anything given, done or suffered; to make amends; or to pay damages.

Do you remember what King Abimelech said when he restored Sarah back to Abraham? "'Look my kingdom over, and choose the place where you want to live'...Then he turned to Sarah. 'Look'...'I am giving your "brother" (Abraham) a thousand silver pieces as **damages** for what I did, **to compensate for any embarrassment and to settle any claim** against me regarding this matter. **Now justice has been done'"** (Genesis 20:15–16 TLB emphasis mine).

Even though he ignorantly took Sarah into his house, the king knew that he had to pay damages and compensate Abraham and Sarah for any embarrassment that he caused. Until he did, justice was not complete.

Another story of divine recompense is when God delivered the children of Israel from Egypt. God not only wanted the children of Israel delivered from bondage, He also wanted Pharaoh to pay damages—400 years' worth of damages! Pharaoh was going to pay damages to one generation for everything suffered during 400 years of slavery.

The Lord tells Moses, "And I will give this people favour in the sight of the Egyptians: and it shall come to pass, that, when ye go, ye shall not go empty: but every woman shall borrow of her neighbour, and of her that sojourneth in her house, jewels of silver, and jewels of gold, and raiment: and ye shall put *them* upon your sons, and upon your daughters; and ye shall spoil the Egyptians" (Exodus 3:21–22).

God not only released the Israelites from bondage but gave them divine favor. This favor caused the wealth of the Egyptians, which included silver and gold, fine jewelry, beautiful clothes, and all kinds of costly goods, to transfer into the hands of God's people. God made sure that the Israelites were recompensed for their suffering.

"The hand of the Lord" is mentioned in several places throughout the Bible. Each time the hand of the Lord moved, there was a blessing on one side and curses or judgment on the other side. This is what happened when the hand of the Lord moved on Pharaoh to release the children of Israel.

God tells Moses, "But Pharaoh shall not hearken unto you, that I may lay my hand upon Egypt, and bring forth mine armies, *and* my people the children of Israel, out of the land of Egypt by great judgments. And the Egyptians shall know that I *am* the Lord, when I stretch forth mine hand upon Egypt, and bring out the children of Israel from among them" (Exodus 7:4–5).

The people of God went free, and they took the spoil of the Egyptians without a fight. They found favor in the sight of their enemies to receive all that they had. That is divine recompense!

The Unjust Judge and the Hand of the Lord

In Luke, chapter 18, Jesus is teaching His disciples "that men ought always to pray, and not to faint" (verse 1) and uses a parable about an unjust judge.

> "There was a judge in a certain city," he said, "who neither feared God nor cared about people. A widow of that city came to him repeatedly, saying, 'Give me justice in this dispute with my enemy.' The judge ignored her for a while, but finally he said to himself, 'I don't fear God or care about people, but this woman is driving me crazy. I'm going to see that she gets justice, because she is wearing me out with her constant requests!'" Then the Lord said, "Learn a lesson from this unjust judge.

A Right View of Vengeance and Recompense

Even he rendered a just decision in the end. So don't you think God will surely give justice to his chosen people who cry out to him day and night? Will he keep putting them off? I tell you, he will grant justice to them quickly! But when the Son of Man returns, how many will he find on the earth who have faith?" Verses 2–8 NLT

I read about a court case in New York City during the Great Depression that reminded me of this unjust judge in Jesus' parable. The judge's name was Judge Lewis J. Smith, and George Baker was the man on trial in his courtroom. Most people today would know Baker by the name of Father Divine. Although Father Divine is controversial in many religious circles still today, I found the account of his legal trial compelling enough to put in this book. For those who have never heard of George Baker, aka Father Divine, let me share a brief background.[24]

George Baker rose to fame and international attention at a time "when Blacks were getting hanged from trees and when the average white person (in America) was barely surviving...New York City was in total chaos."[25] The account goes on, "Grown men...were reduced to standing in food lines waiting for morsels of bread and rice. The mood in New York, as well as in the nation, went from confusion to frustration to desperation."[26]

Now enters Father Divine, a short (less than five feet tall), bald black man with a "squeaky voice who tells people 'God wants you to have money.'"[27] The author writes, "In those days, to preach that God wants you

Vengeance of the Lord

to have money was not only unheard of, it could be considered blasphemy and could get a preacher thrown out of the pulpit."[28]

Father Divine started an organization called the Peace Mission, and by the mid-1930s, it was the largest property owner in Harlem.[29] It owned 25 restaurants, six grocery stores, ten barber shops, and a coal business with three trucks, just to name a few businesses.[30] It is reported that "his members owned 700 separate businesses in New York and New Jersey, as well as thousands of acres of farmland."[31]

Not surprisingly, Father Divine's prosperity and prominence angered many of his not-so-prosperous neighbors who "launched a campaign to destroy him."[32] The New Jersey District Attorney's office tried to sexually entrap Divine with a "Samson and Delilah technique," but it failed. Public officials then turned to running Divine out of the city. Residents living near the Peace Mission called police to complain that Divine's services were disturbing the peace.[33]

Police arrested all of Divine's followers and made them each pay a five-dollar fine. Then, about 1,000 residents gathered at a local high school to reveal that a white woman was in Divine's movement.[34] Mixing of the races at that time was considered a social and cultural anathema, and in some places it was illegal. Father Divine was indicted for "disturbing the peace, fraudulent solicitation and moral charges."[35]

A Divine Day in Court

Father Divine was brought before Judge Lewis Smith in May 1932. Smith was described as the "sternest,

A Right View of Vengeance and Recompense

meanest, unmerciful, racist judge you could possibly imagine."[36] The charges against Father Divine included holding religious services at which large numbers of colored and white people mingled together.[37] Here is a snapshot of their interaction.

> "What is the source of your wealth?" A cold morbid 'I hate you' tone was in the judge's voice. "God," replied Father Divine. The word *God* seemed to have a paralyzing effect on the courtroom. The audience was transfixed on Divine and the judge. It was the ultimate showdown, like watching two heavyweight boxers stare into each other's eyes. But in this case, it was a greater fight; the rightness of man's law vs. the righteousness of God's law. The shock of hearing God's name in a legal arena made it so quiet you could hear two ants kissing.[38]

Judge Smith repeated his question two more times and Divine repeated his answer unflinchingly. "God," he told the judge. Enraged, Judge Smith railed at Divine accusing him of trying to embarrass him in his own courtroom. The all-white jury sentenced Divine to one year in jail and a $500 fine.[39] But, that was not the end of the story.

Three days after he sentenced Father Divine to jail, Judge Smith "grabbed his chest, kneeled over and died of a heart attack right on the floor of his courtroom."[40] Another account of Judge Smith's death said that he died four days later at his home. "At midnight, the justice woke his wife complaining of chest pains....but by the time the doctor arrived, Justice Lewis J. Smith, fifty-five, had died of a heart attack."[41]

Father Divine's only response upon hearing about the judge's death was, "I hated to do it." He was then released prematurely from jail..."The trial, Judge Smith's death and Father Divine's early release from prison gained him respect over America and in many parts of the world."[42]

The Story of David, Abigail and Nabal

The Bible gives a precedent for what happened to Judge Smith in 1 Samuel, chapter 25. Nabal was a very rich man who had many possessions including 3,000 sheep and 1,000 goats. Although he was wealthy, the scriptures also say that he "was rough and evil in his doings." His wife's name was Abigail, "a woman of good understanding, and beautiful."

When David heard that Nabal was shearing his sheep, he sent ten of his men to ask Nabal for assistance:

> I hope that you and your family are healthy and that all is going well for you. I've heard that you are cutting the wool from your sheep. When your shepherds were with us in Carmel, we didn't harm them, and nothing was ever stolen from them...My servants are your servants, and you are like a father to me. This is a day for celebrating, so please be kind and share some of your food with us. Verses 6–8 CEV

Nabal rebuffs David's request, saying, "Who does this David think he is? That son of Jesse is just one more slave on the run from his master...What makes you think I would take my bread, my water, and the meat that I've had cooked for my own servants and give it to you?" (verses 10–11).

Nabal's response infuriated David who told 400 of his men to grab their swords because he was going to avenge himself against Nabal and his entire household. Fortunately, one of Nabal's servants told Abigail what had happened and she quickly gathered food and supplies to give to David and to ask for his forgiveness for Nabal's transgression. Abigail's wisdom worked and David retreated from the harm he was intending to do.

But look how the story ends for Nabal.

> Abigail went back home and found Nabal throwing a party fit for a king. He was very drunk and feeling good, so she didn't tell him anything that night. But when he sobered up the next morning, Abigail told him everything that had happened. Nabal had a heart attack, and he lay in bed as still as a stone. Ten days later, the LORD took his life. David heard that Nabal had died. "I praise the LORD!" David said. "He has judged Nabal guilty for insulting me. The LORD kept me from doing anything wrong, and he made sure that Nabal hurt only himself with his own evil." Verses 36–40 CEV

Ecclesiastes 8:11 KJ21 says, "Because sentence against an evil work is not executed speedily, therefore the heart of the sons of men is fully set in them to do evil." But Jesus reminds us in Luke, chapter 18, "And shall not God avenge His own elect, who cry day and night unto Him, though He bear long with them? I tell you that He will avenge them speedily" (verses 7–8 KJ21).

An End-Time Revelation

When the vengeance of the Lord is first taught, some Christians get quiet. They haven't been taught in this way about God's protection. But vengeance and recompense is a revelation from the heart of God. I also believe it is the single most important revelation for a born-again, Spirit-filled believer to know after learning how to walk by faith. Why? Because in these last days, we cannot complete our kingdom assignment—the work that God has given us to do on the earth—without it.

This revelation of the Lord's vengeance requires spiritual maturity on the part of the believer. In the book of Ezekiel, the Lord says, "Say unto them, *As* I live, sayeth the Lord God, I have no pleasure in the death of the wicked; but that the wicked turn from his way and live..." (Ezekiel 33:11). God wants "all men (and women) to be saved, and to come unto the knowledge of the truth" (1 Timothy 2:4).

We must always remember that vengeance doesn't work outside of love. Moses could not hate Pharaoh. Daniel could not hate King Nebuchadnezzar. And you can't hate whoever has hurt or mistreated you. God sees everything, and He will repay.

Chapter 5

Your Harvest is Crying Out

The book of James describes a powerful end-time prophetic event about the vengeance of the Lord in the last days. In this prophecy, His vengeance is specifically directed against economic injustice, and it is the first time in the New Testament that God refers to Himself with His Hebrew name, Jehovah Tsaba, or Lord of Sabaoth in the Greek.[43]

The *Lord of Sabaoth* means "the Lord of Hosts." Who are the hosts? God's angel armies.[44]

This is what James prophesied:

> Come now, ye rich men, weep and howl for your miseries that shall come upon you. Your riches are corrupted and your garments moth eaten. Your gold and silver are cankered, and the rust of them shall be a witness against you and shall eat your flesh as it were fire. Ye have heaped treasure together for the last days.
>
> Behold, the hire of the laborers who have reaped your fields, which you kept back by fraud, crieth; and the cries of those who have

reaped have entered into the ears of the Lord of Sabaoth. James 5:1–4 KJ21

Verse 4 in the *Amplified Bible* says, "Look! The wages that you have [fraudulently] withheld from the laborers who have mowed your fields are crying out [against you for vengeance]; and the cries of the harvesters have come to the ears of the Lord of Sabaoth."

Notice, <u>two cries</u> are coming up to God's ears: one from **the wages** crying to get into the hands of their rightful owners, and the other from **the laborers** waiting to receive their overdue wages. What are they crying out for? The vengeance of the Lord.

I heard a minister teach this passage in James 5 in the context of seedtime and harvest. He said that many people in the Body of Christ have sown financial seed into the kingdom of God, but they have not yet received the harvest due to them. He said, "You have sown seed and your harvest belongs to you, but satan is holding it." Satan is a thief and a deceiver, and so are the spiritual forces under his demonic control.

Satan doesn't want believers to receive their harvest because he knows that when they do, their faith in God's law of sowing and reaping will have "proof" and they will continue to give to the gospel. This is why the devil hates testimonies, especially of healings and financial breakthroughs. Miracles are evidence to the unbeliever that faith in Jesus and God's Word is able to bring heaven to earth.

Sharing the gospel, eradicating poverty, feeding the hungry and advancing God's kingdom in every nation takes money and lots of it. That is why the psalmist said that God has "pleasure in the prosperity of His servant" who "favor (His) righteous cause" (Psalm 35:27 AMPC).

The speaker went on to say that believers must be "aggressive harvesters." We must enforce the release of our harvest, not from God because He has already promised it, but from the kingdom of darkness. This is why Jesus said, "And from the days of John the Baptist until now the kingdom of heaven suffereth violence, and the violent take it by force" (Matthew 11:12). The MEV translation says, "From the days of John the Baptist until now, the kingdom of heaven has forcefully advanced, and the strong take it by force."

Commanding Casseroles in Jesus' Name

I shared an example of spiritual forces holding back the revenues of a Christian business owner in my book *Faith and the Marketplace*. His company, located in Europe, was on the brink of disaster because customer orders for his pots and casserole pans had seemingly dried up. The closing of his factory seemed like the only solution until God, the Lord of Sabaoth, stepped in. Here is an excerpt of his story.

> Our sales figures were automatically logged as we were linked with major department stores and received their orders as the computers logged the sales. Our daily output was approximately 3,000 casserole pans, and this was very satisfactory.
>
> However, by May there were no new orders, and so I contacted the customers asking them what was wrong. They simply reassured me that everything was fine and orders would be coming

in. But towards the end of the month we had only received $700 USD worth of sales. Virtually nothing. I was deeply troubled.

Again we phoned the customers to check, but meanwhile, the warehouse was filling up with casseroles. As I surveyed the crowded warehouse I knew there was nothing else I could do. Production had to be stopped. Our customers had confirmed that nothing was wrong, and yet orders were drying up.

I prayed, spoke to Asther (my wife), and told her that there was nothing more we could do. The factory would have to be closed if we were to survive the crisis.[45]

He shared that he and his wife went to a prayer meeting that night and heard a woman share Leviticus 26:8 NIV, "Five of you will chase a hundred, and a hundred of you will chase ten thousand, and your enemies will fall by the sword before you." He became encouraged and shared his problem with the prayer group. They began to pray…"we took authority in the name of Jesus Christ and commanded those casseroles to move out and give glory to God!"[46]

The prayer meeting was on a Friday evening. On Monday morning he said his office manager met him on the stairs and said, "Good news! I guess we should praise the Lord! Some of our major customers called and they've bought everything we have except the one litre and three litre casseroles. They want us to ship the order today."[47] The businessman said they quickly began filling the customers' orders until he remembered that this was not the total answer to their prayer. They had commanded all the casseroles to sell and give glory to God. He wrote:

> I called the office manager into my room and shared the situation with him...Surely we needed to agree that the remainder went as well? So in unity, now with the office manager, we prayed once more. This time we specifically spoke to the one litre and three litre casseroles to obey the command![48]
>
> He said within thirty minutes the phone rang with a customer desperately seeking one and three litre casseroles to be shipped immediately. "Our entire stock left the warehouse in one day."[49]

You Have Angels

We are not alone in enforcing satan to release our harvest. God has given us supernatural help in the form of angels. God has assigned to every believer "harvesting angels" to help defeat the spiritual forces holding back their harvest; however, angels only hearken to the voice of the Lord. If we are not speaking God's Word over our harvest, or worse, saying words against what God has already said about our finances (e.g., "Oh, I'll never get these bills paid."), then we bind the angels from moving on our behalf. Psalm 103:20 says, "Bless the LORD, ye his angels that excel in strength, that do his commandments, hearkening unto the voice of his word."

God also warns us not to provoke our angels:

> Behold, I send an Angel before thee, to keep thee in the way, and to bring thee into the

place which I have prepared. Beware of him, and obey his voice, provoke him not; for he will not pardon your transgressions: for my name *is* in him.

But if thou shalt indeed obey his voice, and do all that I speak; then I will be an enemy unto thine enemies, and an adversary unto thine adversaries. For mine Angel shall go before thee.... Exodus 23:20–23

If you are not crying out for your harvest, satan will try to hold it back by fraud or deception. *To cry* means "to make a loud utterance in protest or opposition demanding immediate action."[50] The deception is that satan tries to convince believers that they are not entitled to a harvest, that God forgot about them, or focus on what others will think of them if they become rich. If you don't believe that money belongs to you, then you will not demand God's vengeance and recompense.

Remember the story of Jacob and his uncle Laban in the book of Genesis? Jacob fell in love with Laban's younger daughter, Rachel. Laban promised Rachel to him if Jacob would work for him for seven years. Well, Jacob did, but when the time came to wed Rachel, Laban tricked Jacob into marrying Leah, Rachel's older sister. Jacob then had to work another seven years to win the woman of his dreams. "And ye know that with all my power I (Jacob) have served your father. And your father hath deceived me, and changed my wages ten times; but God suffered him not to hurt me" (Genesis 31:6–7).

Finally, Jacob cried out to God, who gave him a supernatural plan to free himself from Laban's indentured servitude. "And the angel of God spoke unto me in a dream, saying, 'Jacob!' And I said, 'Here am I.' And he said, 'Lift up now thine eyes and see: all the rams which leap upon the animals are ring streaked, speckled, and grizzled; for **I have seen all that Laban doeth unto thee"** (Genesis 31:11–12 KJ21 emphasis mine). God sees all that satan has done to us, stolen from us, or kept back by fraud!

God Is a God of Justice

> For I, the LORD, love justice. I hate robbery and wrongdoing. I will faithfully reward my people for their suffering and make an everlasting covenant with them. Isaiah 61:8 NLT

So, God took away Laban's flocks and gave them to Jacob... "And the man increased exceedingly and had large flocks, and maidservants and menservants, and camels and asses" (Genesis 30:43 KJ21). The transfer of wealth from Laban to Jacob was so staggering that Laban's sons said, "Jacob has taken away all that was our father's; he has acquired all this wealth *and* honor from what belonged to our father" (Genesis 31:1 AMPC).

A speaker at one of our business conferences, a Christian real estate entrepreneur, shared his personal encounter with the vengeance of the Lord in the early days of his real estate business.[51] His powerful testimony demonstrated the victory that comes when we have unrelenting faith in God's justice system.

Our speaker had partnered with a very wealthy businessman who he called George (not his real name) on a successful commercial real estate deal.

Unfortunately, George was also dishonest and deceitful. When the time came for George to pay our speaker his share of the profits, more than a half million dollars, he decided he simply was not going to pay him what was rightfully owed. This profit meant the survival of our speaker's new company.

Although the law was on our speaker's side, he knew that suing George was not an option. Because George had much deeper financial pockets, he could keep them tied up in litigation for years—draining our speaker's finances and eventually destroying his new business. He saw no way of winning **except he believed that God was a God of justice**.[52]

He prayed to God about the situation and surrendered the battle to Him. Once he did, he received the confidence that God would fight the battle against George. He also knew that he had to fight against the spirit of fear, which he did by praising and worshipping God.

The Lord instructed our speaker to call George every week, which he did for ten weeks, and calmly ask him about his payment. Each time George refused. During their tenth telephone call, George became very angry and said that he was going to fly to our speaker's hometown and tell him to his face that he was never going to pay him the money. A meeting was arranged, and the two met a week later at the local airport.

As they entered an airport conference room, our speaker said he didn't know what to say so he decided to keep quiet and hold his peace. As they sat down opposite one another, he said something strange began to happen. Instead of looking at him, George kept staring at something over our speaker's head.

All of a sudden, the color drained from George's face as if he were going to have a heart attack. Our speaker said he was about to ask George if he was okay, but the Lord spoke to his heart not to speak. God was handling this. In obedience, our speaker said he held his peace and kept quiet. "The LORD shall fight for you, and ye shall hold your peace" (Exodus 14:14).

As they sat at the table, George's shoulders suddenly began to slump, as though the Lord had drained every bit of resistance and arrogance out of his body. George then started trembling and weakly mumbled, "We will pay you." Two days later, our speaker checked his bank account online and found there had been a wire transfer for the half million dollars he was owed.

So, what happened? As our speaker said, "My best guess is that He (God) opened George's eyes into the spirit realm and let him see either the angel that stood guard over me or a glimpse of the Lord Himself."[53]

Again, God said in Ezekiel 33:11 that He has no pleasure in the death of the wicked, but that they turn from their evil ways. I believe God gave George the opportunity to "repent" or change his wicked decision, and if he had not, he might have died in that airport conference room.

Invoking Vengeance

If you have been waiting on an overdue harvest, begin to cry out for your harvest and do it with authority! I don't care if it is from a seed that you sowed ten or twenty years ago. It belongs to you! Demand justice, in Jesus' Name! Say Psalm 118:25 out loud right now, "Save now, I beseech thee, O LORD: O LORD, I beseech thee, send now prosperity."

As a blood-washed child of God, you have authority over the devil and God's Word spoken in authority is the only kind of talk to which satan responds. Always remember that when dealing with the devil, you cannot keep silent. Speaking words, filled with faith, is an absolute requirement in invoking the vengeance and recompense of the Lord. You cannot stay silent! Words initiate your authority in the earth and enforce the covenant of God in your marriage and family, your business, your community and your nation. To help you get started, there are three prayers in the back of this book for you to pray <u>out loud</u>: a vengeance prayer for individuals and families, a vengeance prayer for church growth and a vengeance prayer for business.

Let the Lord of Sabaoth, the God-of-the-Angel-Armies, bring economic vengeance for every harvest that satan has stolen or held back by fraud and deception. Like Jacob, God can give you a dream, a business idea or a creative invention that will produce millions of dollars. You may not know how God is going to prosper you, but you can know that He will. Your job is to believe it and speak it!

The Supernatural Wealth Transfer

The book of James also reveals what will happen in the last days to wealthy people who choose to remain outside of God's covenant and continue to serve the kingdom of darkness and themselves with their riches:

> Come [quickly] now, you rich [who lack true faith and hoard and misuse your resources], weep and howl over the miseries [the woes, the

judgments] that are coming upon you. Your wealth has rotted and is ruined and your [fine] clothes have become moth-eaten. Your gold and silver are corroded, and their corrosion will be a witness against you and will consume your flesh like fire. You have stored up your treasure in the last days [when it will do you no good].
James 5:1–3 AMP

Throughout the Old Testament, God promised that great wealth from the Gentiles (those who don't know God) would be transferred into the hands of His people. "This *is* the portion of a wicked man with God, and the heritage of oppressors, *which* they shall receive from the Almighty. If his children be multiplied, *it is* for the sword: and his offspring shall not be satisfied with bread. Those that remain of him shall be buried in death: and his widows shall not weep. Though he heap up silver as the dust, and prepare raiment as the clay; he may prepare *it*, but the just shall put *it* on and the innocent shall divide the silver" (Job 27:13–17).

One man wrote, "Through an abundant access (transfer) of the wealth of the wicked Gentile world," God would show His glory to the world.[54] The Old Testament books of Isaiah, Haggai and Zechariah have significant portions of scripture related to this transfer of wealth from the hands of the wicked into the hands of the righteous.

Isaiah, chapter 61, which Jesus partly quoted in Luke, chapter 4, says, "The Spirit of the Lord God is upon me, Because the Lord has anointed *and* commissioned me To bring good news to the humble *and* afflicted…To proclaim the favorable year of the Lord, And the day of vengeance *and* retribution of our God, To comfort all who mourn" (verses 1–2 AMP).

Isaiah goes on to say, "Then they (God's people) will rebuild the ancient ruins, They will raise up *and* restore the former desolations; And they will renew the ruined cities, The desolations (deserted settlements) of many generations" (verse 4 AMP).

Also in Isaiah, chapter 60, God says, "Arise, shine; for thy light is come, and the glory of the Lord is risen upon thee...And the Gentiles shall come to thy light, and kings to the brightness of thy rising...the forces of the Gentiles shall come unto thee...they shall bring gold and incense; and they shall shew forth the praises of the Lord...and I will glorify the house of my glory" (verses 1, 3, 5–7).

The prophet Haggai also makes reference that the latter house (the end-time Church) will be greater than the former house.

> I will shake all the nations; and they will come with the desirable *and* precious things of all nations, and I will fill this house with glory *and* splendor,' says the Lord of hosts.
>
> 'The silver is Mine and the gold is Mine,' declares the Lord of hosts.
>
> 'The latter glory of this house will be greater than the former,' says the Lord of hosts, 'and in this place I shall give [the ultimate] peace *and* prosperity,' declares the Lord of hosts. Haggai 2:7–9 AMP

As one man wrote, "You can see from these verses that God's purpose in visiting an economic vengeance upon the Gentile world is necessary for the economic comfort that is to come upon the Christian."[55] Didn't Isaiah 61 say God would "comfort all who mourn"? Imagine what the Church can accomplish with billions of dollars. "If you are willing to link yourself up with almighty God as your source, all the wealth of the world may be placed at your unlimited disposal"[56] and position you to "become a greater influence in the world for goodness and God's righteous cause."[57]

Now you can see why it's so critical to see yourself far above the world and satan. You are not a victim! There is work to do and God has chosen you to do it! We're in the set time of God's vengeance. The Church will move in such power and wealth that it will stagger the imagination of the world.

Chapter 6

Why We Need Vengeance

> But when Daniel learned that the (*ungodly*) law had been signed, he went home and knelt down as usual in his upstairs room, with its windows open toward Jerusalem. He prayed three times a day, just as he had always done, giving thanks to his God. Daniel 6:10 NLT

Out of envy and greed for power, Daniel's coworkers tricked the king into passing an unjust law that required Daniel to dishonor God or face certain death. As verse 10 reveals, Daniel refused to obey the law and continued to pray openly three times a day, giving thanks to God.

What gave Daniel the courage to continue following God without compromise? A revelation of God's justice.

One of the main reasons for vengeance is for you to be able to stand for righteousness in the midst of an ungodly system, and to be confident that you will not get hurt and that you will change the system to which you have been sent.

"Being sent" is part of your kingdom mandate. It means that God will use you to bring light where there is darkness; to provide influence to guide nations back to God; and to take kingdom jurisdiction over your specific domain, thereby bringing all laws, ordinances, codes, statutes and executive actions in line with the government of God. All these things, including systems, institutions, legislations, regulations and policies, will be brought in line to accommodate our divine purpose.

> Say unto God, How terrible *art thou in* thy works! through the greatness of thy power shall thine enemies submit themselves unto thee. Psalm 66:3

Christians must know the level of power that redemption has conferred upon them. Satan only submits to power. Vengeance empowers believers to take an uncompromising stand against evil and injustice as they establish God's kingdom.

There are evil powers constantly working to stop the plan of God and frustrate your assignment. And, as shared in an earlier chapter, one of the main responsibilities of the Holy Spirit is to execute judgment upon all the enemies of God's people and nothing (spiritual or physical) shall escape Him.

The apostle Paul, by the unction of the Holy Ghost, invoked a curse on the sorcerer Elymas.

> And now, behold, the hand of the Lord *is* upon thee, and thou shalt be blind, not seeing the sun for a season. And immediately there fell on him a mist and a darkness; and he went about seeking some to lead him by the hand. Acts 13:11

The devil will go to almost any length to keep you from fulfilling your assignment. Paul was moved by the Holy Ghost and God executed vengeance on this man who was using witchcraft to stop the spread of the gospel.

The vengeance of the Lord is part of God's promise to execute judgment upon all forces visible and invisible, resisting the full expression of our redemptive rights. God promised Abraham that, "I will bless them that bless thee, and curse him that curseth thee: and in thee shall all families of the earth be blessed" (Genesis 12:3). This promise includes every born-again child of God!

Your redemptive rights are everything Jesus died to provide and return back to mankind…health, peace, protection, financial soundness and prosperity, blessed marriages, happy families, authority and dominion.

This "Believers' Bill of Rights" and blessings have been given to us through our redemption in Christ… "according as his divine power hath given unto us all things that *pertain* unto life and godliness,…" (2 Peter 1:3).

> Christ hath redeemed us from the curse of the law, being made a curse for us: for it is written, Cursed *is* every one that hangeth on a tree. Galatians 3:13

The apostle Paul gave an encouraging word to the Corinthian church and all believers when he wrote:

> The grace of the Lord Jesus Christ, and the love of God, and the communion of the Holy Ghost, *be* with you all. Amen. 2 Corinthians 13:14

As I defined in an earlier chapter, the word *communion* is from the Greek word *koinonia* meaning "partnership and responsibility." The Holy Spirit wants to become your partner. He wants to assume a greater responsibility for you in this world. He's our Helper, our Advisor, and now our Protector. He will deal with anyone or anything resisting you from receiving and enjoying your redemptive rights in Christ through the vengeance of the Lord!

Here are two other important reasons why every believer in the Body of Christ needs the vengeance of the Lord.

Vengeance Brings Supernatural Breakthroughs

> And the LORD said unto Moses, Yet will I bring one plague *more* upon Pharaoh, and upon Egypt; afterwards he will let you go hence: when he shall let *you* go, he shall surely thrust you out hence altogether. Exodus 11:1

Without the vengeance of the Lord, the children of Israel and their descendants would have remained in bitter slavery. So, God sent Moses, His prophet, to deliver them from Pharaoh's bondage, and only the "plague of vengeance" was powerful enough to humble Pharaoh to let God's people go. Through God's vengeance, Pharaoh had to bow to God's will and authority and was made to realize that his earthly throne was no match for the power and sovereignty of God's.

God's vengeance also brought supernatural deliverance through the hands of Esther. God chose Esther to become queen in a heathen nation, and He anointed her "for *such* a time as this"; that is, to stand up against an evil leader and an evil law seeking to wipe God's people off the face of the earth.

In the book of Esther, the Jews faced certain genocide at the hands of Haman, the king's right-hand man, and like Moses, Esther was chosen to deliver them.

> And Haman said unto king Ahasuerus, There is a certain people scattered abroad and dispersed among the people in all the provinces of thy kingdom; and their laws *are* diverse from all people; neither keep they the king's laws...
>
> If it please the king, let it be written that they may be destroyed:.... Esther 3:8–9

Mordecai, Queen Esther's cousin, sent her a message to intercede on behalf of her people before the king. But for Esther to do this meant risking her own life. There was a law that whoever approached the king without being invited would be put to death. The only exception was if the king extended his golden scepter.

Esther told Mordecai to gather all the Jews and tell them to fast for three days and nights and she would go to the king, which she did. After a series of divinely orchestrated events, Haman was hanged on the gallows that he had built for Mordecai and Haman's property was given to Esther. The king also passed a law that protected all the Jews:

> In it the king granted the Jews who were in every city *the right* to assemble and to defend their lives; to destroy, to kill, and to annihilate

any armed force that might attack them, their little children, and women; and to take the enemies' goods as plunder,.... Esther 8:11 AMP

Here is the final reason we need God's vengeance.

Vengeance Guarantees the Completion of Your Assignment and That You Will Reach Your God-Ordained Destiny

As shared in earlier chapters, vengeance is required for every believer to complete what God has called them to do on Earth for the gospel and the kingdom of God. The Holy Spirit and angels have been assigned to help us reach our God-given destiny. As said before, "When the Church has not invoked vengeance or when the Church is ignorant of vengeance then we become victims."

Someone may ask, "Victims of what?" Victims of the devil's deceptions to frustrate and harass us, and his schemes to drain our energy and steal our dreams. We were never designed to fight our own battles!

There are places on this earth that are so dark and demon-controlled that they can't be reached without the vengeance of the Lord clearing the way.

Jesus said, "For these be the days of vengeance, that all things which are written may be fulfilled" (Luke 21:22).

It took vengeance to free Israel from the bondage of Egypt, and only through vengeance was Moses able to return to Egypt and take his place in history. "...the Lord said unto Moses in Midian, Go, return into Egypt: for all the men are dead which sought thy life" (Exodus 4:19).

In the New Testament, all those who sought to kill baby Jesus were wiped off the face of the earth. Hear what the Lord told Joseph in Matthew, chapter 2:

> But when Herod was dead, behold, an angel of the Lord appeareth in a dream to Joseph in Egypt, saying, Arise, and take the young child and his mother, and go into the land of Israel: for they are dead which sought the young child's life. Verses 19–20

Notice that only a few years had passed because the scriptures say that Jesus was still a young child. God's judgment was executed quickly (See Ecclesiastes 8:11) so that God's prophetic agenda could be completed.

Chapter 7

Not a Martyr But a Savior

Years ago when I was employed full-time at a major computer corporation in sales, I was doing very well. One day my manager asked to see me in his office where he shared with me about a call that he had received from one of our company's prospective customers. This company had recently been assigned to me as one of my new accounts. After I had made my first visit to the company, one of the executives called my manager to say that he didn't want an African American handling his account.

My boss asked me, "Bill, what shall I do about this." I said, "Well, why don't you give the account to someone he can accept, someone other than an African American." He responded, "You don't really mean that?" I said, "Sure. Just give me another opportunity of equal value."

I realized that some people still had problems from a racial standpoint. But, I was determined not to let their problem become my problem. Being born again as a believer, I had gotten beyond the victim mentality, and I knew that no one could stop me from reaching my goals but me. That same year I was the number one salesman in the Chicago downtown branch office. I knew that whatever God had planned for me, that if I walked by faith, practiced truth and stayed in the love of God, I could not be defeated.

Now, after I became a sales manager in the company, I experienced a brief setback. God was miraculously causing business to come into my sales unit even when the economy was at a major all-time low. I was walking by faith and sowing seed...and nothing could abrogate my harvest. The Bible says, "They will not be ashamed in the time of evil, and in the days of famine they will have plenty *and* be satisfied" (Psalm 37:19 AMP). People didn't know how I was getting all this business, but I knew. I was using the principles of the kingdom of God.

My boss wanted to promote me, so he selected me to be part of a presentation to several company executives who had flown in from New York and Atlanta. I didn't know it, but my participation in the presentation was strategically planned for them to take a look at me as a candidate for a higher level position within the company.

That's when the situation happened. A day or two before I was to present, another African American in the company started sharing with me his list of grievances about all the unfair things the company was doing to him. And, without knowing it, I took on that same victim mentality. I became angry at the company for what I thought they were doing to my co-worker. I stepped out of faith and God's love and emotionally wanted to retaliate. Remember, VENGEANCE IS NOT REVENGE. Revenge is a principle of the kingdom of darkness, along with hatred, witchcraft, division, greed, threats, etc. They all work to bring destruction. As Galatians 5:21 AMP says, "those who practice such things will not inherit the kingdom of God." For the believer, God fights our battles.

As a result of taking on this negative, victim mindset, the meeting went terribly. My attitude was absolutely reprehensible during the entire presentation. I acted like I didn't want to answer any questions...it was awful. The scriptures warn us, "Do not be deceived: 'Bad company corrupts good morals'" (1 Corinthians 15:33 AMP). This plainly says to watch your associations.

The meeting was so bad that my boss came into my office after the guests had left and used some very aggressive language about what I did. He told me that they were there to observe me and to decide whether or not to promote me and bring me on to their staff. Wow, did I feel bad. I eventually somewhat recovered from my mistake, but it took a while.

So what happened? I was like Moses in a way. I tried to get revenge. (See Exodus 2:11–13.) And, you could say... <u>I struck the rock</u>. Listen to what Moses said in frustration to the people he was leading, "Hear now, ye rebels; must we fetch you water out of this rock?" (Numbers 20:10). Resentment and emotional retaliation cost both of us. It cost Moses his job and the destiny God had planned for him. He never got into the Promised Land.

I let my emotions overrule my kingly righteousness, and I sunk to the level of the world in terms of revenge. And, it cost me. I'm saying this because we have to make a clear difference between revenge, which is a principle of darkness, and vengeance, which is void of hate or emotional resentment. If we don't, we will not succeed. We have to understand that.

We also have to understand that vengeance protects us. If vengeance is understood and believed, it guarantees the protection of your mind, your body and all that you have (family, material possessions, etc.). It's designed to do that. Jesus said, "I lay my life down." Why? Because no one could kill Him, the same as they can't kill you or make you fail in your earthly assignment.

From the writing of the Constitution of the United States of America, we have always been "One nation under God." Now the phrase "under God" is under attack. The enemy is slowly working to take God out of the United States of America. So it is up to the Church to contend with him and repossess the ground he illegally occupies. To do that, we must clearly understand the vengeance of the Lord and that no weapon formed against us will prosper. When we stand against ungodly laws having to do with freedom and the ungodly principles of a demon-controlled world, we must know that we win every battle and that we will always return safely, untouched and unshaken.

Everything that is not lined up with the government of the kingdom of God must be brought back into divine alignment. It says in Isaiah 9:7 NLT,

> His government and its peace will never end. He will rule with fairness and justice from the throne of his ancestor David for all eternity. The passionate commitment of the Lord of Heaven's Armies will make this happen!

This means that nothing can stop God's government from spreading. But we must believe this!

We are not to be like Esther. Somehow Esther felt that she could get away without manifesting her "salt" (Matthew 5:13–16) and God's plan for her to "make history" in saving a nation. So, she began to make excuses, "I am fearing for my life to go before the king without being called." Her cousin Mordecai had to help Esther get back in faith for God's protection and vengeance by saying,

> Do not imagine that you in the king's palace can escape any more than all the Jews. For if

you remain silent at this time, liberation and rescue will arise for the Jews from another place, and you and your father's house will perish [since you did not help when you had the chance]. And who knows whether you have attained royalty for such a time as this [and for this very purpose]? Esther 4:13–14 AMP

The Bible says God Himself will put the fear of you upon them (the enemies of God). That's what happened with the four lepers who decided not just to sit and wait but to go into the enemy's camp. And when they got there, God had made the enemy to hear noises, and they became afraid and fled, leaving everything including food and gold. God can give the ungodly what to think. He gave Esther favor with the king.

The Bible says God reigns over the heathen.

God reigneth over the heathen: God sitteth upon the throne of his holiness. Psalm 47:8

And said, O LORD God of our fathers, *art* not thou God in heaven? and rulest *not* thou over all the kingdoms of the heathen? and in thine hand *is there not* power and might, so that none is able to withstand thee? 2 Chronicles 20:6

We cannot neglect our purpose for being here on this earth—to "be fruitful, and multiply, and replenish the earth, and subdue it" (Genesis 1:28). Jesus said we are to be "salt," and "being salt" sometimes puts us in a place of confrontation. In the case of Dr. Martin Luther King, Jr., his campaign for justice put him in a place that was life-threatening, and he eventually was shot and killed. We will forever honor him and all those who have given their lives for the cause of freedom and justice in any and every nation.

However, I challenge you, according to God's promise for our deliverance, not to think for one moment that this has to happen to you. The Scriptures tell us,

> No weapon that is formed against thee shall prosper; and every tongue *that* shall rise against thee in judgment thou shalt condemn (Isaiah 54:17), and

> A thousand shall fall at thy side, and ten thousand at thy right hand; *but* it shall not come nigh thee. Only with thine eyes shalt thou behold and see the reward of the wicked. Psalm 91:7–8

Jesus: Not a Martyr But Our Savior

Some people have thought of Jesus as a martyr, but He wasn't. He is our Savior. And that's why He died. No one could take His life. He could have had twelve legions of angels rescue Him (Matthew 26:53), the same as Elisha (2 Kings 6:16–17), and the same as you. Jesus "gave up the ghost." Why? So that you and I could live and have dominion over death.

If you look at the last chapter of the book of Acts, the last two verses reveal how the apostle Paul lived at the end of his life.

> And Paul dwelt two whole years in his own hired house, and received all that came in unto

him, preaching the kingdom of God, and teaching those things which concern the Lord Jesus Christ, with all confidence, no man forbidding him. Acts 28:30–31

Paul preached the gospel freely with no man hindering him. We have to understand that the vengeance of the Lord guarantees the believer's safety and preservation. Understanding this will bring God's full protection no matter what situations we get into. Yes, we are in a war against the kingdom of darkness; however, we are not to become martyrs but to win the battles God sends us to fight, returning with our lives intact. Numbers 32:20–22, often called the "Soldier's Prayer," confirms this,

> And Moses said unto them, If ye will do this thing, if ye will go armed before the Lord to war, and will go all of you armed over Jordan before the Lord, until he hath driven out his enemies from before him, and the land be subdued before the Lord: **then afterward ye shall return, and be guiltless before the Lord**, and before Israel; and this land shall be your possession before the Lord. (Emphasis mine.)

I firmly believe that significant changes are coming in the United States of America…like religious freedom in our public schools; true prison reform where people are rehabilitated and have their full rights restored including their records expunged after they've paid their time; or whatever else that is in the earth that is out of line with God's government and kingdom culture.

Again, like Moses, like Esther, like Daniel and like Paul, we have a place and a mission that at times could put us in a place of personal danger. But Jesus Himself said,

> These things I have spoken unto you, that in me ye might have peace. In the world ye shall have tribulation: but be of good cheer; I have overcome the world. John 16:33

> I have told you these things, so that in Me you may have [perfect] peace *and* confidence. In the world you have tribulation *and* trials *and* distress *and* frustration; but be of good cheer [take courage; be confident, certain, undaunted]! For I have overcome the world. [I have deprived it of power to harm you and have conquered it for you.] John 16:33 AMPC

Conclusion

> Strengthen ye the weak hands, and confirm the feeble knees. Say to them *that are* of a fearful heart, Be strong, fear not: behold, your God will come *with* vengeance, *even* God *with* a recompence; he will come and save you. Then the eyes of the blind shall be opened, and the ears of the deaf shall be unstopped.. Isaiah 35:3–5

As I wrote in the book's introduction, we are living in a set time when the kingdom or government of God will be established throughout the earth. It's a time when every spiritual force that has been assisting the ungodly against God's end-time army of believers will now be put down. "But the Lord shall arise upon thee, and his glory shall be seen upon thee...because the abundance of the sea (rich sea trade and wealth of nations) shall be converted unto thee...Therefore thy gates shall be open continually; they shall not be shut day nor night; that *men* may bring unto thee the forces (riches, wealth and resources) of the Gentiles" (Isaiah 60:2, 5, 11).

The devil has been using spiritual forces to win, to humiliate, to persecute, devastate and harass God's people. His mission of wickedness has kept the children of God from possessing their inheritance, reaching their destiny and fulfilling God's commission: advancing His kingdom throughout the earth. No natural man without God can defeat them. Only faith and those who are empowered by the Holy Spirit can overcome the demonic forces of darkness and halt their work of wickedness among people and nations—and not be touched.

> Say unto God, How terrible *art thou in* thy works! through the greatness of thy power shall thine enemies submit themselves unto thee. Psalm 66:3

Spiritual Forces of Darkness

Satan, the invisible world of evil spirits and the demon-controlled world system are the real enemies of all human beings. These are the principalities that rule the dark world. They bring evil into this world mainly through suggestions of evil thoughts, words and deeds to those people who allow themselves to be influenced by them. These spirits, when allowed, invade and possess humans who, when in leadership, eventually make evil, ungodly rules, regulations and laws that are against God's laws and take control of all the goods and services in the world.

God told Moses about these demon-driven nations in Exodus, chapter 23, and said that He would send His angel to defeat them.

> For mine Angel shall go before thee, and bring thee in unto the Amorites and the Hittites, and the Perizzites and the Canaanites, the Hivites and the Jebusites: and I will cut them off.

> Thou shalt not bow down to their gods, nor serve them, nor do according to their works: but thou shalt utterly overthrow them and quite break down their images. Verses 23–24 KJ21

Conclusion

The Amorites, Hittites, Perizzites, Canaanites, Hivites and Jebusites were spiritual forces, each with certain characteristics (strong men) occupying the land, who were resisting the children of Israel from possessing their Promised Land, and they are still in the earth today. Satan still uses these spiritual forces today to oppose or frustrate and win over God's redeemed and I believe that knowledge of God's vengeance has been the missing piece. God said through His prophet Hosea, "My people are destroyed for lack of knowledge" (Hosea 4:6). The fact that we are born again does not give us automatic access to our inheritance in the kingdom of God. No! You have to take it by faith, exercising your dominion mandate in every arena of life. Jesus said, "The violent take it by force."

Understand that invisible battles come in different forms, but mostly as spells and sorcery or enchantment. The root behind certain issues is curses or forces that are provoked by some demonic source that is responsible for those issues.

> As the bird by wandering, as the swallow by flying, so the curse causeless shall not come.
> Proverbs 26:2

A curse needs a cause to come into a life, a family or a nation, and satan is the one that enforces the curse. We can see an example of this in the life of Job. Through wrong words, Job tore down the invisible hedge that protected him. Finally, after many sorrows, he cried out to God and said, "Teach me, and I will hold my tongue: and cause me to understand wherein I have erred," (Job 6:24).

> The wicked is [dangerously] snared by the transgression of his lips, but the [uncompromisingly]

righteous shall come out of trouble. Proverbs 12:13 AMPC

Although spiritual forces of wickedness are real, God does not intend that any spell or enchantment have any effect on our lives.

> Surely *there is* no enchantment against Jacob, neither *is there* any divination against Israel: according to this time it shall be said of Jacob and of Israel, What hath God wrought! Numbers 23:23

Another translation says, "No curse can touch Jacob..." (NLT).

When Moses and Aaron confronted Pharaoh, they were also confronting the witchcraft and magic that Pharaoh relied upon to rule Egypt, "Then Pharaoh also called the wise men and the sorcerers: now the magicians of Egypt, they also did in like manner with their enchantments. For they cast down every man his rod, and they became serpents: but Aaron's rod swallowed up their rods" (Exodus 7:11–12 emphasis mine). God's spiritual forces of light will always triumph over the forces of darkness.

Jesus delivered every born-again child of God from the curse, and any enchantment and spell sent from the kingdom of darkness. Galatians 3:13–14 says:

> Christ hath redeemed us from the curse of the law, being made a curse for us: for it is written, Cursed *is* every one that hangeth on a tree:
> that the blessing of Abraham might come on the Gentiles through Jesus Christ; that

Conclusion

we might receive the promise of the Spirit through faith.

We must have the faith of God to invoke the presence of God for our deliverance, whether we need God's mercy or God's vengeance, in opposing the wicked.

For example, as I shared in an earlier chapter, the Lord's judgment came upon Elymas, the sorcerer, when he tried to use his demonic witchcraft power to block Sergius Paulus, the deputy (governor) of Paphos, from hearing the Word of God.

> Then Saul, (who also *is called* Paul,) filled with the Holy Ghost, set his eyes on him, and said, O full of all subtilty and all mischief, thou child of the devil, *thou* enemy of all righteousness, wilt thou not cease to pervert the right ways of the Lord?
>
> And now, behold, the hand of the Lord *is* upon thee, and thou shalt be blind, not seeing the sun for a season. And immediately there fell on him a mist and a darkness; and he went about seeking some to lead him by the hand. Acts 13:9–11

Notice how the Holy Spirit will execute the vengeance of the Lord. Even though Paul spoke it, the Holy Ghost orchestrated it. In these last days, the Lord is sending us into places where we are the "salt of the earth" and the "light of the world." Understanding vengeance will remove all fear and turn us from victims to victors. The same as He did with Moses when God sent him to confront the most powerful government of that day... the Pharaoh of Egypt. It took vengeance for Moses to take his place and succeed at his mission. Faith in the vengeance of the Lord is a vital aspect of our success in these final days.

The apostle Paul says, "For we wrestle not against flesh and blood, but against principalities, against powers, against the rulers of the darkness of this world, against spiritual wickedness in high *places*" (Ephesians 6:12). Our fight today is between the forces of darkness and the children of light. Guaranteed, there will be a confrontation. The scriptures tell us, "For the devil is come down unto you, having great wrath, because he knoweth that he hath but a short time" (Revelation 12:12). Well, I can imagine he would be a little upset as the wealth and people begin to flow from his kingdom into the kingdom of God's dear Son. Just the same as Pharaoh, who was furious when the children of Israel marched out of Egypt with all the people and the wealth, protected by God.

In the last days, the darkness will become darker and the wickedness will become more wicked. But, we have a more powerful answer to this darkness. It's called light. And we have a more powerful answer to the wickedness. It's called the vengeance of the Lord. It will silence any opposition and make wickedness bow at your feet, in Jesus' Name.

> For the day of vengeance *is* in mine heart, and the year of my redeemed is come. Isaiah 63:4

> For I the LORD love justice; I hate robbery *and* wrong with violence or a burnt offering. And I will faithfully give them their recompense in truth, and I will make an everlasting covenant *or* league with them. Isaiah 61:8 AMPC

Conclusion

In essence, God is "comforting Zion," His people. For anything that is shameful, afflicted, humiliating... there is an anointing (latter rain) of restoration, which includes the vengeance and recompense of the Lord, to turn it around. Vengeance, like faith and love, is in the Word of God and putting it to work guarantees your triumph. God spoke to Abraham at the beginning of his journey:

> And I will make of thee a great nation, and I will bless thee, and make thy name great; and thou shalt be a blessing: and I will bless them that bless thee, and curse him that curseth thee: and in thee shall all families of the earth be blessed. Genesis 12:2-3

The *Amplified Bible, Classic Edition* says it this way:

> And I will make of you a great nation, and I will bless you [with abundant increase of favors] and make your name famous *and* distinguished, and you will be a blessing [dispensing good to others].
>
> And I will bless those who bless you [who confer prosperity or happiness upon you] and curse him who curses *or* uses insolent language toward you; in you will all the families *and* kindred of the earth be blessed [and by you they will bless themselves]. Genesis 12:2-3

It is our redemptive right, when prompted by the Holy Ghost, to execute judgment upon the wicked. Not out of hate for them, but out of love for justice. Realize, it is done by faith and faith works by love. Love is not a feeling. Love is God, and He works through us by faith to engage in violent judgment or vengeance upon all forces, seen and unseen, which would dare resist us or rob us of our redemptive rights.

God's Economic Vengeance

For every born-again believer, our redemption is not complete without divine provision. Currently, the world system controls most of what is needed to meet human need, which is almost everything, from the drug industry (medicine) and healthcare to elite educational institutions to baseball teams (sports and entertainment).

Without enough money, people in the world have no options. God's people live by faith. And God intended for His people (the Church) to be the distribution center of the world, not secular governments or the heathen rich. What a powerful tool to turn the world back to God!

As the apostle James prophesied in James, chapter 5, the wicked wealthy will be silenced by God's vengeance (the Lord of Sabaoth) against the Babylonian world system. This economic vengeance is part of God's promise to comfort His people in the last days. "For the Lord shall comfort Zion: he will comfort all her waste places" (Isaiah 51:3).

We Have Heaven's Authorization

Let the high *praises* of God *be* in their mouth, and a twoedged sword in their hand; to execute vengeance upon the heathen, *and* punishments upon the people;

Conclusion

> to bind their kings with chains, and their nobles with fetters of iron; to execute upon them the judgment written: this honour have all his saints. Praise ye the Lord. Psalm 149:6–9

This passage says that we have heaven's authorization to invoke vengeance upon the wicked and all those being sent by the devil to thwart our purpose or delay God's plan. It took the vengeance of the Lord to protect baby Jesus when Herod, being insanely wicked, ordered the execution of all children who were two years and under living in Bethlehem. God had warned Joseph in a dream to flee with Mary and the child to Egypt.

The Scriptures then tell us,

> But when Herod was dead, behold, an angel of the Lord appeareth in a dream to Joseph in Egypt, saying, Arise, and take the young child and his mother, and go into the land of Israel: for they are dead which sought the young child's life. And he arose, and took the young child and his mother, and came into the land of Israel. Matthew 2:19–21

Notice, Jesus was still a "young child" and Herod and all those who sought the child's life had died…or I might say, were judged by the hand of the Lord. Again, nothing and no one escapes when the vengeance of the Lord takes over. More than once God says, "For the battle *is* not yours, but God's" (2 Chronicles 20:15). Also, recall that God said; quoting Ezekiel 33:11: "I have no pleasure in the death of the wicked; but that the wicked turn from his way and live."

Because God's people have not had a revelation of vengeance, they have remained under torment and without a testimony. However, those days are over. God says, "for he that toucheth you toucheth the apple of his eye" (Zechariah 2:8). The CEV translation says, "Whatever you do to Zion (the Church), you do to him (God)." And faith is the only way to execute this benefit of God's vengeance to step in and overthrow all the evil and wicked forces coming against us. I decree that after reading this book, your days of being robbed, afflicted, harassed and depressed and your promises delayed are all over, in Jesus' Name! Expect only that which is good from this day forward!

Vengeance Prayer for Individuals and Family

Oh Lord our God; the Most High God; Maker of heaven and earth; our Creator, our Sustainer, and our Protector. You are the just God of all the earth sitting on Your throne of judgment in the high court of heaven. You, Lord, execute righteousness and justice for all that are oppressed. You are the Lord of the Sabaoth, the Ruler over all, and the God of angelic armies that fight against our enemies and avenge us of our adversaries. Beside You, there is no Savior. Because of Your great love toward us and Your love for justice, You forsake not Your saints, but You come to our aid to uphold the justice upon Your throne in heaven.

    Father, I lift my life and my family up to You, declaring that it is Your set time of favor. The enemy has been oppressing Your children. He has been resisting us. But now, Lord, we call upon You to dismantle everything that is out of line with heaven's government in our lives. Hear our cry, oh Lord! Be gracious and hearken to us. Restore justice and judgment in all of our situations. For You love righteousness and You hate wickedness. Bring Your righteous judgment upon our adversary and against all that he is doing. Punish and penalize him for what he has put us through—every suffering, every humiliation, every shame, every embarrassment, every loss, every entrapment, every sickness, and every attack of the devil. He is the perpetrator; he is behind all injustices, and I pray, in the Name of Jesus, deal with him and deliver us out of every affliction. Restore everything he has stolen from us and our ancestors and everything delayed; bring it forth now in this season.

I command the release of inventions, opportunities, discoveries, businesses, organizations, ministries, industries, creative ideas, relationships, contracts, awards, promotions, wealth, inheritances, and all the increase that has been fraudulently held up, misdirected, sabotaged, blocked, stolen, and destroyed.

Execute Your vengeance against this enemy speedily and bring to us the full recompense that is due to us as redeemed heirs of God and joint heirs with Christ, that we may advance Your kingdom in all of the earth. Crush the oppressor and all wickedness and establish Your justice in my life and my family. I ask and receive it by faith, in the Name of Jesus. Amen!

Vengeance Prayer for Church Growth

Father God, in the Name of Jesus, we decree Your vengeance upon every agent of the devil resisting the continuous growth of our church. We destroy every plan and purpose of hell against our church growth agenda for the year. We decree destruction upon every work of the devil and his armies engaged in opposition against the commanded blessing of the Lord, thereby releasing divine increase and an invasion of multitudes attending all of our services. Crowds are being born into the kingdom of God in unprecedented numbers and fulfilling their heavenly mandate for earthly dominion.

Father, in the Name of Jesus, and by the Blood of the everlasting covenant we decree vengeance upon all the gods of the land resisting the continuous influx of record-breaking multitudes into our church. Let the fire of God descend to consume the demonic agents of the devil wherever they gather to plan any hurt against this church and its individual members or our staff. Father, in the Name of Jesus, plead the cause of this church and fight those that fight against her continuous growth. We decree the destruction of every spell, curse, and enchantment against the glorious destinies of our new converts and members in this church this year.

We decree judgment upon all satanic activities targeted at stalling the growth of this church. Father, silence all evil counselors that seek to dissuade potential converts from coming to Christ, being established in this church, and established in the faith. We call forth supernatural multiplication throughout this year. Lord God, be an enemy to our enemies and an adversary to our adversaries.

We destroy all satanic oppression sent against us, and we command freedom and perpetual deliverance from all wickedness for our members and staff. May signs, wonders and miracles confirm the Word that is preached. Father, give Your angels charge over us to keep, defend and preserve us in all of our ways.

Lord, we thank You for exceeding our expectations and growing Your church supernaturally as we release our faith. Let supernatural breakthroughs occur in every service, member and staff worker this year. We count it all joy and decree that we reap and keep every new convert, and disciple them to be mighty ambassadors that will advance the kingdom and glorify You, in Jesus' Name, amen!

Vengeance Prayer for Business Growth

Father, I come boldly to Your throne of grace lifting my business up to You. I thank You for the grace and the anointing to do business Your way, and I decree that You are the Lord my God, that is teaching me how to profit, and leading me in the way that I should go.

I decree Your vengeance upon every agent of the devil resisting the continuous growth and success of my business, and let the effect be evident in our annual revenues and day-to-day operations. Father, I destroy every plan and purpose of hell against my business, and I decree null and void every plot of principalities and powers against the success of my business endeavors.

Lord, arise and scatter every confederacy and demonic assault against the continuous growth and profitability of my business. I decree destruction to every power of darkness on assignment against my business and declare that the gates of hell will not prevail. I plead the Blood of Jesus over my business and decree that no weapon formed against it will prosper. Silence every tongue that rises up to speak against the prosperity of Your servant, my organization, my staff and partners.

Thank You, Lord, that You are blessing the works of my hands and increasing us daily. My business is flourishing, a beacon of light in the industry and I am distinguished and dominating in my sphere of influence.

I call forth customers and clients, employees and partners, and all that will assist in marketing and promoting the brand of the organization. I decree my business is a catalyst for the wealth transfer, and I believe and receive it by faith.

Thank You that we operate according to the biblical principles and far exceed the standard that is in this world. Father, I receive Your wisdom, revelation knowledge, counsel and might to lead and to operate the business with integrity that will influence and transform the world. Thank You, Lord, for giving me innovative strategies and solutions to offer as products and services that create value and draw wealth and riches. I decree that I am always in the right place, at the right time, with the right information, and the right understanding. I discern my harvest, and I always gather it. I praise You, Lord, that my business not only launches but continues to increase and expand supernaturally.

Lord, cause Your face to shine on me and on my business and give us favor with You and with man. I decree that everything that pertains to the start-up and expansion of this business has come to me in abundance. Lord, open my eyes to see new opportunities and increase my discernment. Lead me by Your Spirit, and make me sensitive to hear Your voice.

My trust and hope is in You, Lord. And, I thank You that You are causing all grace to flow to me and this business in abundance. Execute Your divine vengeance on behalf of my business, and cause every obstacle, hindrance, and blockage to cease immediately in Jesus' Name. I decree that (name of your business) is a successful kingdom business that glorifies You, in Jesus' Name, amen.

William (Bill) Samuel Winston

Bill Winston is the visionary founder and senior pastor of **Living Word Christian Center** in Forest Park, Illinois.

He is also founder and president of **Bill Winston Ministries**, a partnership-based global outreach ministry that shares the gospel through television, radio, and the internet; the nationally accredited **Joseph Business School** which has partnership locations on five continents and an online program; the **Living Word School of Ministry and Missions**; and **Faith Ministries Alliance (FMA)**, an organization of more than 600 churches and ministries under his spiritual covering in the United States and other countries.

The ministry owns and operates two shopping malls, **Forest Park Plaza** in Forest Park and **Washington Plaza** in Tuskegee, Alabama. Bill Winston is also the founder and CEO of **Golden Eagle Aviation**, a fixed base operator (FBO) located at the historic Moton Field in Tuskegee.

Bill is married to Veronica and is the father of three, Melody, Allegra, and David, and the grandfather of eight.

Books By Bill Winston

- Born Again and Spirit Filled (Available in English, Polish and Spanish versions)
- Climbing Without Compromise
- Divine Favor – A Gift from God, Expanded Edition
- Faith & The Marketplace
- Imitate God and Get Results (Available in English and French versions)
- Possessing Your Mountain
- Power of the Tongue
- Seeding For the Billion Flow
- Supernatural Wealth Transfer: Restoring the Earth to Its Rightful Owners
- Tapping the Wisdom of God
- The God Kind of Faith, Expanded Edition
- The Kingdom of God In You: Discover the Greatness of God's Power Within
- The Law of Confession: Revolutionize Your Life and Rewrite Your Future with the Power of Words
- The Missing Link of Meditation
- The Power of Grace
- The Power of the Tithe
- The Spirit of Leadership: Leadership Lessons Learned from the Life of Joseph
- Training For Reigning: Releasing the Power of Your Potential
- Transform Your Thinking, Transform Your Life: Radically Change Your Thoughts, Your World, and Your Destiny
- Vengeance of the Lord: The Justice System of God

Connect With Us!

Connect with Bill Winston Ministries on Social Media. Visit www.billwinston.org/social to connect with all of our official Social Media channels.

Bill Winston Ministries
P.O. Box 947
Oak Park, Illinois 60303-0947
(708) 697-5100
(800) 711-9327
www.billwinston.org

Bill Winston Ministries Africa
22 Salisbury Road
Morningside, Durban, KWA Zulu Natal 4001
+27(0)313032541 orders@bwm.org.za
www.bwm.org.za

Bill Winston Ministries Canada
P.O. Box 2900
Vancouver, BC V6B 0L4
(844) 298-2900
www.billwinston.ca

Prayer Call Center
(877) 543-9443

Endnotes

[1] "The power of the wicked is always enhanced by the timidity and indecision of the righteous." Quote attributed to Sir Winston Churchill by Henry Kachaje, "When Good People Commit Gross Crimes by Remaining Silent," *Afriem.org* (blog), May 29, 2014, http://www.afriem.org/2014/05/good-people-commit-gross-crimes-remaining-silent/.

[2] *1828 Edition of Noah Webster's American Dictionary of the English Language* online, s.v. "recompense," accessed September 17, 2018, http://1828.mshaffer.com/d/search/word,recompense.

[3] Dr. Martin Luther King, Jr., "I Have A Dream" (speech), transcript, *FOXNews* online; FOXNews.com, http://www.foxnews.com/us/2013/08/27/transcript-martin-luther-king-jr-have-dream-speech/#ixzz2dIMiXW5s (hereafter cited as King, "I Have A Dream").

[4] Bill Winston, *Faith & the Marketplace*, (Oak Park, IL: Bill Winston Ministries, 2016), page 152 (hereafter cited as Winston, *Faith & the Marketplace*).

[5] Emmett J. Scott and Lyman Beecher Stowe, *Booker T. Washington: Builder of a Civilization*, (Garden City, NY: Doubleday, Page & Company, The Outlook Publishing Co., 1916) page 117.

[6] Ibid., page 117.

[7] Ibid., page 118.

[8] Ibid., page 118.

[9]Ibid., page 118.

[10]Rick Williams, with Jared C. Crooks, *Christian Business Legends* (Ashland, OH: Business Reform and The Business Reform Foundation, 2004), page 37.

[11]Ibid., page 37, quoted from George Grant, Lecture on Booker T. Washington, (Moscow, Idaho: Canon Press, 2000) Cassette tape.

[12]Ibid., page 40.

[13]James Strong, *Strong's Exhaustive Concordance of the Bible* "Hebrew Chaldee Dictionary, (Nashville, TN: Thomas Nelson Publishers, 1990), in *Strong's Hebrew Lexicon*, ref 892, "babah," Hebrew translation for "apple."

[14]"Koinónia." Greek translation for "partnership," accessed September 17, 2018, *Strong's Exhaustive Concordance of the Bible* "Greek Dictionary of the New Testament," ref. 2842, https://biblehub.com/greek/2842.htm.

[15]Jose Martinez, "Hundreds Protest Across America in Response to Charlottesville Violence," Complex.org, Complex Media, August 13, 2017, https://www.complex.com/life/2017/08/charlottesville-protests-across-america.

[16]King, "I Have A Dream."

[17]Anthony Ray Hinton with Lara Love Hardin, *The Sun Does Shine* (New York, NY: St. Martin's Press, 2018), front cover inside flap.

[18]Ibid., page 166.

[19]Ibid., page 228.

[20]Ibid., page 238.

[21]Press article, "Case of spanking preacher thrown out," *RNW.org Media*, RNW archives, Radio Netherlands Worldwide,

Endnotes

accessed September 26, 2018, https://www.rnw.org/archive/case-spanking-preacher-thrown-out.

[22] Ibid.

[23] Ed Silvoso, *Transformation: Change the Marketplace and You Change the World* (Ventura, CA: Regal Books, 2007), page 116.

[24] K.P. Spraggins, *Great Black Money Makers: African Americans Who Made Fortunes* (Harvey, IL: C & K Enterprises, 1998), page 64 (hereafter cited as Spraggins, *Great Black Money Makers*).

[25] Ibid.

[26] Ibid.

[27] Ibid.

[28] Ibid.

[29] Ibid., page 65.

[30] Ibid.

[31] Ibid.

[32] Ibid., page 67.

[33] Ibid.

[34] Ibid., pages 67–68.

[35] Ibid., page 68.

[36] Ibid.

[37] Ibid.

[38] Ibid., page 69.

[39] Ibid.

[40] Ibid., page 70.

[41] Jill Watts, *God, Harlem U.S.A. The Father Divine Story* (Berkeley and Los Angeles, CA: University of California Press, 1992), page 97, quoted from *Suffolk County News* (*SCN*), June 10, 1932, 1; *Nassau Daily Review*, June 9, 1932, reprinted in *The New Day* (*ND*), August 31, 1974, 17.

[42] Spraggins, *Great Black Money Makers*, page 70.

[43] Dr. Don G. Pickney, *A Prosperity Phenomenon* (Lake Mary, FL: Creation House, A Charisma Media Company, 2012), page 107 (hereafter cited as Pickney, *A Prosperity Phenomenon*).

[44] Ibid., page 16.

[45] Winston, *Faith & the Marketplace*, page 78.

[46] Ibid.

[47] Ibid., page 79.

[48] Ibid.

[49] Ibid.

[50] Savelle, Jerry. "2018 Southwest Believers' Convention: Sowing in Famine (7:00 p.m.)." Filmed August 2, 2018. SWBC video, 1:15. Posted August 3, 2018. https://www.youtube.com/watch?v=AhRwz9GMk-w.

[51] Michael Galiga, guest speaker, Economic Empowerment Summit," (EES 2010), Living Word Christian Center, Forest Park, IL, November 2010.

[52] Michael Galiga, *Win Every Battle* (Minneapolis, MN: Bronze Bow Publishing, 2009) pages 61–71.

[53] Ibid., page 71.

[54] Pickney, *A Prosperity Phenomenon*, page 2.

[55] Ibid., page 133.

[56] Ibid., page 7.

[57] Ibid.